SUPER-POWERED ASTROLOGY

PRAISE FOR *SUPER-POWERED ASTROLOGY*

"As with music, making poetic connections between the infinite possibilities of notes, making songs out of the zodiac has the power to illuminate an individual's path. Gifted at her instrument, Jill Dearman is the astrologer of our collective future. Through *Super-Powered Astrology*, you will find your voice and the confidence to use it to rock the world into a state of magical revolution."

—Melissa Auf Der Maur, Hole/ The Smashing Pumpkins (Pisces)

"I didn't know a ton about astrology, which is why it was wonderful to have Jill Dearman explain it in a way that I could understand. *Super-Powered Astrology* reveals why we act the way we do and provides down-to-earth guidance for creating a better life and better world, all with the help of the stars!"

—Jeff Hiller, Emmy-winning actor, *Somebody, Somewhere* (Sagittarius)

"I love *Super-Powered Astrology*! Jill Dearman rides the new wave of astrology into the future. Her witty and culturally savvy style, coupled with a practical approach to metaphysics, brings the stars down to earth. What fun, and useful too! She ties the change of signs of Uranus, Neptune, and Pluto to personalized tools for development in a unique application of astrology. And the melding of tools like the I Ching, Kabbalah, and Tarot is ultra-cool as well."

—Rick Levine, *Astrology Hub Podcast* (Aries)

"The cosmic superhero antidote to our Bizarro world!"

—Dean Haspiel, Emmy & Ringo Award–winning cartoonist, creator of *The Red Hook* (Gemini)

"Wondering what the stars have in store for you? Wonder no more. Jill Dearman's *Super-Powered Astrology: Four Steps to a New You for a New Astrological Age* will give you everything you need to know in order to maneuver smoothly and safely through the new cosmic order. Unlike other books on astrology, *Super-Powered Astrology* reveals the remarkable abilities and potentials unique to each sign, from the visionary talents of Aquarius to the shamanistic skills of Scorpio. The new age ahead may seem daunting, but with Dearman as a guide, the outlook is good, whatever your sign."

—Gary Lachman, author *The Secret Teachers of the Western World* (Capricorn)

SUPER-POWERED ASTROLOGY

Four Steps to a New You for a New Astrological Age

JILL DEARMAN

Countryman Press

An Imprint of W. W. Norton & Company
Independent Publishers Since 1923

This book is a general information resource about how to use astrology to try to identify and achieve personal goals. **The information in this book does not constitute and should not be construed as psychological, psychiatric, medical, financial, legal, or any other kind of professional advice on any subject.** Please use your judgment about when to seek out advice from a licensed professional for your particular needs. In particular, if you are experiencing significant physical pain of any kind, even if you think the cause may be emotional or psychological, consult a physician or other healthcare provider immediately.

Astrological signs on page 4: Nazarii / iStock; Astrological signs on chapter openers: urbazon / iStock; masks throughout text: IRYNA NASKOVA / iStock; Superhero bursts throughout text: Natallia Prachova / iStock; Hebrew letters: Olena Poliakevych / iStock; I Ching Hexagrams: iSidhe / iStock

Printed in the United States of America
First Edition

Manufacturing by Lakeside Book Company
Book design by Beth Steidle
Production manager: Devon Zahn

Countryman Press
www.countrymanpress.com

An imprint of W. W. Norton & Company, Inc.
500 Fifth Avenue, New York, NY 10110
www.wwnorton.com

Authorized EU representative: EAS, Mustamäe tee 50, 10621 Tallinn, Estonia

978-1-324-11206-8

10 9 8 7 6 5 4 3 2 1

For Phe

CONTENTS

PROLOGUE

Superheroes and Astrology: The Origin Story

As a preteen I had two obsessions: comic books and astrology. Every day after school, I would go down to the stationery store around the corner on Queens Boulevard to experience the glory of time standing still as I thumbed the circular carousel of comic books. Batman and Superman were the superheroes I spent the most time (and quarters) on. My parents were divorced, and on Saturdays I would go with my father—a New York City cab driver who lived in the Bronx—to used comic book stores and expand my collection.

It wasn't until many years later that an uncanny coincidence showed me a connection between my two passions. I was on way home from my office at The Writers Room in downtown Manhattan on a rainy Friday evening and decided to stop at the Strand bookstore on Broadway and 12th Street. It was there that I came upon a book in the Philosophy and Eastern Thought section, hidden away in the basement. It was titled *An Unlikely Prophet: A Metaphysical Memoir by the Legendary Writer of Superman and Batman*, by Alvin Schwartz. In it, the writer from the Golden Age of Comics tells of a late-in-life experience he had that placed him on a spiritual path. (He still ate pastrami sandwiches, though, so he didn't go too crazy!)

He recounted that he had a literal visit from a Tibetan Buddhist of questionable material form. Through their strange conversations, Schwartz came to realize that Superman was more than just a character, but a "tulpa"—a materialized thought form—he had brought into actual existence. The concept of the tulpa emerged from Tibetan Buddhists. They believed these beings in human shape could manifest in the material world through intense concentration and spiritual connection.

Interestingly, Schwartz was the writer who invented a superfoe of Superman's called Bizarro, first introduced in 1958. Inspired by Swiss psychologist Carl Jung's concept of "the shadow," Bizarro is as strong as Superman but lacks his conscience. Bizarro entered the mainstream vernacular in the '90s by way of a couple hilarious episodes of *Seinfeld*.

The original comic book idea of a "Bizarro World" was a place that appeared like ours but embodied the opposite values. Polarized as our planet is now almost 70 years later, it seems the one thing we all can agree on is that the world feels upside down, as if we are living on a Bizarro planet. During these times we desperately need superheroes, and they are not going to come from the sky or the screen or from the comic books of my youth. They have to start with us: our thoughts, beliefs, and imaginations.

When I do astrological charts, I always tell clients that I follow a "character as destiny" model. In other words, it doesn't matter if someone has the potential to be a table tennis star, an architect, or a comic book artist—what matters is the energy and belief they put into it. Potential will remain just potential unless we focus our attention on a particular area.

Think of it this way: There are infinite versions of each of us that exist in the quantum field. If you want to, let's say, live in Paris instead of Pittsburgh, there is a version of you who is already there, eating a baguette avec fromage in a striped shirt, scarf, and beret. Change can happen swiftly when you focus on aligning your consciousness to another existing reality, rather than plodding through the exhausting physical and material steps you believe you need to take.

Becoming the superhero version of yourself is not about moving matter but aligning with the most powerful and noble version of yourself.

INTRODUCTION

How to Use This Book

Not to begin with a binary, but . . . are we living in a matrix, or has the world just gone completely mad? Sometimes it feels like those are the only two options. Regardless of the answer, one thing is certain: My new brand of astrology can help you make sense of it all and improve your life no matter the outer circumstances. How? By showing you how to navigate the unique landscape of Pluto in Aquarius (2024–2044); guiding you in embodying your inner zodiac superhero, which will help you access your greatest strengths; and setting you up with a fierce and fabulous internal friend group known as your Big-Three High-Vibe Tribe, consisting of your Sun, Moon, and Rising signs.

Let's say you awoke from a dream and realized the dream was real and waking life an illusion. Philosophers, metaphysicists, and kids doing bong hits in college dorms have been asking these questions since time immemorial. Right now, during the second quarter of the twenty-first century, there is growing resurgence in the idea that we are waking up from a collective dream. Even if this belief was a mere illusion, there's still the intriguing fact that at any moment, one-third of the planet is participating in what the Aboriginal people, the early Iroquois, and numerous other native cultures call "the dream time."

Why, even the ultimate goddess, Kate Bush, wrote the title song to her album *The Dreaming* in reverence to the Aboriginal concept. In 1982 she stated, "'The Dreaming' is the time for Aboriginals when humans took the form of animals, when spirits were free to roam and in this song as the civilized begin to dominate, the 'original ones' dream of the dreamtime." For Australian Indigenous people, the Dreaming is part of a cyclical order known as "the Everywhen." In this Everywhen, the ancestors who possess superheroic powers roam the land. Right now, the "when" is a key factor in how we navigate life on earth. The Pluto in Aquarius era calls upon us to wake up and use our astrological superpowers.

In this second quarter of the twenty-first century, it can feel especially difficult to make plans for ten years, five years, or even one year from now because the world has grown so erratic. The veil of security has been torn off, and we can see how high the stakes are for our planet and our species.

What better time than now to turn *inward*? Much like being lost alone in the dark woods, we must use our inner resources to find our way back into the safety and joy of the light. After all, we are spiritual beings having a human experience, not the other way around. Part of the concept of "waking up" is remembering that we are complete as we are, our higher selves know everything, and love is the solution to any problem.

The book will take you through four steps:

THE FOUR STEPS OF SUPER-POWERED ASTROLOGY

Step One

How to Thrive During the Pluto in Aquarius Era

Before traveling to a new land, you might pick up a local guidebook and familiarize yourself with some basic phrases and customs. That's why Step One of this book is dedicated to giving you the lay of the land. Maybe a future book will guide you in getting laid on the land, but let's stay in the moment, shall we?

Step One of *Super-Powered Astrology* gives you context for the chaos we are experiencing from an astrological point of view. In this section, you will learn about the era we have entered into, the Pluto in Aquarius cycle. This era will last for a generation, all the way to 2044—almost as long as *Grey's Anatomy* has been on the air.

Pluto, the planet of power and self-transformation, moved into the radically optimistic, humanitarian, and technology-minded sign of Aquarius full time in 2025. Aquarius, ruled by Uranus, the disruptor planet, sometimes enters situations in shocking, unexpected ways.

Now let's add to this: The progressive planet of Uranus will transit communicative Gemini through 2033, and Neptune, planet of imagination and illusion, will move through bold Aries through 2039. Change is afoot all around!

Based on the astrology of recent years, you have probably already gone through some turbulent times. Transitions are often rocky, and that is certainly the case when major outer planets are changing signs. But once you get the lay of the land and learn the language and customs of Pluto in Aquarius, you just might love it here!

Step Two

Embody Your Superhero Identity

Once you are oriented to the new universe, you can identify your unique role in it. In this section, you will get to know the twelve new zodiac avatars for a world in need of heroes. While Pisces will always be represented by a fish and Libra by a set of scales, these new avatars provide further context for each sign's actionable role in our world—like Pisces the Dreamer and Libra the Artist. After all, you are more than just an overly familiar symbol, you are a superhero! Your new zodiac avatar will inspire you to embody the most expansive, inspiring version of yourself. This superhero avatar leads with its own unique superpower. You will learn how to harness them to find your path, heal yourself, and heal the world. (No big whoop, right?)

Step Three

Collab with Your Big-Three High-Vibe Tribe

You've acclimated to the New World and identified your role in it. Now it's time to make friends!

In this section, you will learn about your Big Three, also known as the unique triad of the Sun, Moon, and Rising signs. There are 1,720 possible combinations, leading to countless distinctive personalities.

Put simply: The Sun sign represents the mind; the Moon sign represents the heart; the Rising sign represents the body.

Platonic friends are more essential than ever in today's world, and so are coaches, guides, and gurus (which happens to be the name of my *woo*-collar law firm). I like to call your Big Three "the High-Vibe Tribe," and I'll help you think of them as your lifelong friends and internal allies. Once you get to know them, you'll feel like you have a whole team on your side.

One of the essential skills of an astrologist is the ability to synthesize the meanings of different chart details and interpret them in a way that resonates and provides guidance. In this section, I will teach you how to do just that for yourself. It is not a formula, but an experiential practice. Much the way astrologists first experiment on their friends and family (it's not like it's brain surgery, right?—insert knife emoji here) to develop insights and intuition, you can become your own astrologist with my guidance. And then, once you're really sure you know what you're doing, you can practice on your peeps and offer knowledgeable astrological support to them.

This section will lay out the twelve Sun signs that rule the mind, the twelve Moon signs that rule the heart, and the twelve Rising signs that rule the body. You will learn how to consult your particular Big-Three High-Vibe Tribe and ask them for situational guidance.

Soon you will integrate the voices of your Big Three into your psyche. You'll be able to synthesize their wisdom yourself. Maybe you'll even discover a concept or a phrase that becomes your port in the storm, your mantra for life.

Step Four

Manifesting Your Dream Life

In this section you will learn to alchemize Steps One, Two, and Three to create your ideal reality. Through exercises a go-go, you will practice the art of synthesizing the cumulative intel to change your life for the better.

To recap: By the end of this book, you will have learned three key pieces of wisdom:

- How to best navigate the 20-year Pluto in Aquarius era
- What your new zodiac superpowers are and how to use them
- How to collaborate with your Big-Three High-Vibe Tribe for wisdom and guidance

By book's end, *you* will be able to discover the powers you've had within you all along and use them to modify your identity and really enrich—and maybe even really *change*—your life. And this method can be applied to any desire, from finding love to getting fit, getting rich, or whatever the wish, great or small. You got this!

An Example of How You Can Use This Book

Suki is working a day job that bores her. It pays well enough but not enough, she feels, to allow it to suck her soul dry! She has a spouse, two kids, and a few chronic health issues. She wants to pursue her goal of being an art therapist but doesn't know how to fit school into such a busy schedule. She also feels too old for that pursuit as she approaches forty. Suki can immerse herself in **Step One** to understand the new astrological era we are entering so she can best figure out a plan to navigate it. Art therapists of the Pluto in Aquarius age are likely to bring new skills to the table, such as more technology and more group-oriented therapy. She can look toward the future rather than the past as she begins considering her options.

Suki is a Virgo, and she could make an immediate goal to practice the exercises in **Step Two** to really embody her superhero self—The Gardener. Suki can lead with her superpower, the power to cultivate, as she works toward her larger goal of becoming an art therapist. Perhaps like a gardener, she can see her goal as akin to growing an apple tree and can then reverse engineer the steps needed to reach that goal. Perhaps she can envision what she would like her life to be like as an art therapist and why she wants to make this her life path. She can grow her business like one would grow a tree, planting the right seeds and providing the tender care required to bring the tree to life.

Suki has Sun in Virgo, Moon in Aries, and Gemini Rising. Using the High-Vibe Tribe described in **Step Three,** she can get practical help from three internal allies. Her Sun sign is Virgo, and the Sun is the "mind" person of the group. Her Moon has the heart of an Aries, and the Rising sign rules the body, signifying her physical self possesses big Gemini energy.

She will begin to develop a simple and helpful practice. If she has a "mind" question or quandary like "How am I going to find the time to even explore the school programs out there?" her practical Virgo Sun can help her figure out the steps to take in the upcoming week. Small goals!

If she has an emotional issue, like "I just don't think anyone would want my help. I'm so insecure," her heart helper, Aries, can assist by teaching her Aries-style confidence-building techniques so she feels more ready to take action.

And if she is grappling with physical challenges, like feeling so fatigued that all she can do is binge prestige television after working all day and taking care of her family, her Gemini Rising can help her with her physical life. Geminis often get energy from laughter, so Suki could seek out something that makes her laugh to start building energy. Geminis are also air signs and very tuned in to breathing, so maybe she will feel encouraged to do just ten minutes of restorative yoga a few times a week to get the ball rolling.

Now that Suki has the different steps mastered, she can learn how to synthesize them all in **Step Four.** This is where she can really focus on manifestation, on the belief that she can make her dreams come true and live in that place of belief. And to quote U2, it's "A place that has to be believed to be seen."

SUPER-POWERED ASTROLOGY

STEP ONE

How to Thrive During the Pluto in Aquarius Era

WELCOME TO A BRAND-NEW WORLD

So what's the big deal about Pluto in Aquarius, and what do you need to know about this era that will last to 2044? Let's break it down. (Drop a beat!) We are all born with a natal chart, which is set from the moment we are born. Within that chart we all have ten planets (including the Moon), each with its own individual influence, in different signs. The chart is split into twelve houses, each of which rules a different area of life, from money to relationships to career and so on. At the time of birth, the planets will land in different signs and houses for each of us based on the astrology of that particular date. The natal chart is a map of the sky at your precise time of birth. It captures the planets and their relationship to each other. Astrologers use this chart to gain insight into your unique personality traits, strengths, challenges, and potential life paths. Think of it as a snapshot of your character at the moment of your birth. If you do not know your time of birth, worry not. The date and city still provide about eighty-five to ninety percent of the information. There will just be a little bit of mystery without that particular data.

In astrology, Pluto rules power and self-transformation. It symbolizes rebirth and holds space for you to emerge into a more self-aware and authentic version of yourself. Perhaps more than any other planet, when it transits your birth chart, it can be fierce and forceful. We all have secrets and shame, but when Pluto comes to town, its purpose is to help you sweat out the toxins, lose your bad habits, and transform your identity from self-destructive to constructive.

Think of Pluto like a tough-love best friend. They can handle your darkness and all your shadows. And if they see you heading for disaster, they're not going to coddle you. For instance, if you keep making the same mistakes about money and hiding your mess out of shame, they may encourage you to own up and take action. This may happen a few times. But when you are finally approaching the point of no-going-back crisis, like a lawsuit or eviction notice, they may give you some real tough love.

Why? Because they know if you just stop avoiding your fears and shame and face them, you can dig yourself out of your hole. And they will be there to help you a hundred percent once you are willing to face what you've been avoiding. All you need to do is take one step, and Pluto will have your back. But if you keep running away, it will stop enabling you—or worse. Pluto has been known to force you to face your bad health habits by giving you an injury to wake you up. It can help you confront your relationship issues by bringing big issues to the fore in disturbing ways, like the sudden chance to move across the country or a flirty interloper inciting drama.

Each planet rules one (sometimes two) signs of the zodiac. Pluto rules Scorpio, thus it has the intense, loyal but intimidating nature of this sign. You can find which sign is ruled by which planet in the chart below.

The Signs and Their Rulers	
Sign	**Planetary Ruler**
♈ Aries	♂ Mars
♉ Taurus	♀ Venus
♊ Gemini	☿ Mercury
♋ Cancer	☽ Moon
♌ Leo	☉ Sun
♍ Virgo	☿ Mercury
♎ Libra	♀ Venus
♏ Scorpio	♇ Pluto
♐ Sagittarius	♃ Jupiter
♑ Capricorn	♄ Saturn
♒ Aquarius	♅ Uranus
♓ Pisces	♆ Neptune

Wherever Pluto is transiting, it's wise for you to get your act together. For example, if it is moving through your house of money and property, pay off some debt and clean your gutters. Once you've taken care of the stuff you've been ignoring, you will have room to deal with what you're hiding from yourself and the world about money. What are you embarrassed about in this area of your life? Bring it into the light and then, I kid you not, you will find the courage and skills to transform your weakness into your strength. After all, when you face your shadows, you no longer have to live in the darkness of fear. How liberating!

In the collective, the lessons of self-transformation are much wider in scope, as you will see below. The point of Step One is to prepare you for being a human in the Pluto in Aquarius epoch—to be in tune with the times and one step ahead. Let's look at the basics of Pluto in Aquarius.

PLUTO IN AQUARIUS: 2024–2044

Aquarius is the sign of technology and progress, the sign of friendship and community. Relationships are already in flux, and the acceptance of open relationships, throuples, platonic partnerships, and more are likely to keep emerging as alternatives to traditional unions.

As we can already see with AI, quantum physics, and the study of consciousness, we are living in the future, making advances at super speed. Even futurist Ray Kurzweil has released a follow-up to his prescient book, *The Singularity Is Near: When Humans Transcend Biology* (2006) with *The Singularity Is Nearer: When We Merge with AI* (2024). We also now have confirmed reports from the CIA and the Pentagon that unidentified anomalous phenomena (UAP) sightings are real. And not a minute too soon! As the Climate Clock ticks and the Earth faces extinction, we need to create the technology to stem the tide or find another planet to live on.

But before we make friends with the aliens, we could use some practice making friends and forming a unified human community with each other. As John Lennon wrote, "You may say I'm a dreamer, but I'm not the only one." This cycle affords us our last best chance to work together as a species to save ourselves, and more than that—to actually ascend to the next level of our spiritual evolution.

Before continuing, it would behoove us to look back at previous Pluto cycles to get a big picture perspective of the planet's influence. And before that, how about a quick note for those with hands raised to ask if Pluto is still a planet?

For astrologists the answer is yes. The same way, for example, a government could theoretically say, "Staten Island is no longer part of New York City. It's not a borough anymore," but that wouldn't necessarily mean forever. (Full disclosure: While riding the S.I. Ferry on my way to a Halloween party in said borough, I concocted the anagram "Satan's Lit Den" for Staten Island. I've tried to convince the powers that be to officially change its name, but no luck so far!)

Similarly, in 2006 a group of astronomers decided Pluto failed to meet updated criteria that defined a planet, and they termed it a "dwarf planet" instead. I guess they dug that phrase as much as I did my anagram! Chances are good that there are still more planets to be discovered in our lifetime and beyond. And chances are Pluto may be called a full planet again. The definition is fluid.

Next you will find insights concerning the past several Pluto cycles, starting with Pluto in Leo.

✵ PLUTO IN LEO: 1938–1957 ✵

Leo is the sign of youthful energy, openheartedness, and charisma. Pluto is the planet that expects us to go through trial by fire and come out the other side renewed. In Leo this plays out as a destruction of parental control and the emergence of the self-expression of the young.

Pluto entered Leo as World War II was being fought and remained there during the postwar years. Suddenly there was a new population boom, and the kids of this period were raised to be thankful for conventional life in the suburbs. They were called the baby boomers. All they had to do was follow convention.

There was only one problem: Leos are born leaders and are not meant to follow the herd.

Leo rules the adolescent time of life, and these rebel souls liked to make their own rules, not listen to old-timers. They did things with passion and in the most public, expressive way possible. As they came of age, boomers brought us a cultural revolution, an anti-war movement, Woodstock, the phrase "sex, drugs, and rock 'n' roll," free expression, and a focus on young people. They may shop at the Gap, play pickleball, and take luxury cruises now, but they were the coolest kids once!

✵ PLUTO IN VIRGO: 1957–1971 ✵

Virgo is a sign associated with a connection to nature and a desire to be of humble service. Pluto, the planet of rebirth, expresses itself in Virgo by reminding us how much our planet and our bodies need our care. The early Gen Xers were born into an era when environmentalism took hold. This cycle included the first Earth Day and the publication of Rachel Carson's *Silent Spring*. This cultural shift aligns with Virgo's values; its concern with the body, the Earth, and nature itself. Virgo also maintains a strong work ethic and a commitment to service. This sign is happy doing the nonglamorous routines that get the job done. When the Pluto in Virgo kids came of age in the '80s, they were confronted with a terrible disease: AIDS. They were right there to provide service to their fellow young people who were dying, and they fought to find the health treatments to save even more from early graves.

PLUTO IN LIBRA: 1972–1983

Libra cares about fairness and letting all sides speak their mind. The way Pluto behaves when it embodies this sign is by leading with a commitment to justice. The time of Pluto in Libra saw justice served against corrupt government during Watergate and the end of Vietnam. The civil rights movement, women's liberation and second wave feminism, and gay rights all converged during this era that demanded equality.

PLUTO IN SCORPIO: 1984–1995

Scorpio is thematically associated with sex and death. Pluto, the planetary ruler of Scorpio, expressed itself with extreme intensity during this cycle. This was the era of AIDS, a disease that was mainly sexually transmitted and for a decade and a half was considered a death sentence. The term "safe sex" became part of the public lexicon, and negotiating intimacy became a life-or-death issue. The year 1995 was the last year of Pluto in Scorpio and the year before protease inhibitor cocktails became available, a turning point in the treatment of HIV, transforming AIDS from a death sentence to a manageable illness. None of this would have happened without years of aggressive activism by the very groups that were suffering most from the illness and their courage in fighting the healthcare system and demanding new treatment.

✵ PLUTO IN SAGITTARIUS: 1995–2008 ✵

Sagittarius is connected with religion and other strongly held beliefs, sometimes to the point of fanaticism. During the middle of Pluto in Sag, we experienced 9/11 and the culture wars. Sag is also thought of as the most garrulous sign in the zodiac. Put those elements together and what does it spell? Talk radio! The culture wars were fought on conservative radio stations. At the same time, everyone got a voice (and a face!) on YouTube and could rant to the converted on personal blogs. These were the times when comedians started advising us on current events. The World Wide Web was also taking hold. With access to new friends from other cultures in faraway lands, thanks to the Internet, citizens had the opportunity to think more globally than past generations.

✵ PLUTO IN CAPRICORN: 2008–2024 ✵

Capricorn loves money and traditional ways to make it. The sign is associated with being cautious and business-savvy. Pluto shows itself in Capricorn by putting the economy at the top of the priority list. This era began with the stock market crash of 2008 and the bailout that followed. Members of Gen Z and Gen Alpha were born into an era when smartphones became accessible and added to the speed of communication but also took away previous expectations of privacy. Were governments monitoring their citizens? Most agree they were and still are! These magical gadgets also meant that work took place at all hours, not just nine to five. And though the United States welcomed its first Black president, blowback came hard with the election of Donald Trump (a reality star of the Pluto in Sag era), Brexit, and right-wing governments throughout the globe refusing to give up power. The COVID crisis exacerbated fear and separation. And the Climate Clock ticked on, back-burnered by the voice of Big Business. This era set the stage for what could be the fall of capitalism and is certainly the call to restructure democracy to make it more democratic and representative. Just remember, the fall precedes the rebuilding.

✵ PLUTO IN AQUARIUS: 2024—2044 ✵

See the first part of this section.

✵ PLUTO IN PISCES: 2044—2067 ✵

Pisces is the planet of endings and new beginnings, psychic phenomena, compassion, and imagination. Looking ahead to the middle of the twenty-first century, what is on the horizon? Pluto in Pisces suggests that there will be an increase in human longevity, with a focus on immortality. There will be progress made in telepathic communication and the music of pure sound frequencies to raise the vibration of the planet. Gen Z and Gen Alpha kids who will be all grown up, we are counting on you!

❋ OTHER PLANETARY TRANSITS ❋

But wait, there's more!

Pluto is not the only planet that is going through epic changes. Uranus and Neptune are as well. Although Pluto will be making the longest transit through a new sign (2024–2044), its neighboring planets are not far behind. During the Pluto in Aquarius epoch, Pluto plays the starring role, as it is the most influential planet. This is because it is farthest from the Sun and takes the longest time to transit the Sun. But let's think of its peers, Neptune and Uranus, as supporting characters in the unfolding story of this era.

Neptune Transit Dates

Neptune entered Aries on **March 30, 2025,** and will remain in the sign of the Warrior until **March 23, 2039**.

What Is Neptune All About?

Neptune is the planet of healing and illusion. This planet is ethereal and ever present, much like our dreams while sleeping and our daydreams while awake. It can fill us with miraculous fantasies that might come true, or delusions that sink us into depression. The former option is more likely if we use our empathy and imagination by helping others and focusing on creativity. The latter option will prevail if we lie to ourselves and succumb to the pull of addiction. It's a fine line.

How Does Neptune in Aries Affect You?

Although the dreamy planet of illusion is decidedly different from the energetic sign of Aries, this combo does make a fascinating mixture.

In Aries, Neptune exhibits much more energy and enthusiasm for its dreams than in other signs. This transit is likely to give us the initiative to take action in support of our dreams. Only when we allow wisdom and empathy to guide us (Neptune) can we break out boldly and take courageous and enthusiastic action (Aries).

Uranus Transit Dates

Uranus entered Gemini on **July 7, 2025,** and will continue its journey through the sign of the Messenger until **May 22, 2033.**

What Is Uranus All About?

Uranus invites us to break our routines, bust out of our comfort zones, and embrace change. Pluto also pushes for change, but it feels more personal. It wants us to deal with our shadows and hidden depths. Uranus is more like a supercomputer. It is supremely logical and strangely neutral. Detached and friendly, it stays focused on its mission of progress. The future is the thing. And Uranus cannot understand or tolerate sticking to the same old patterns that got us into the mess we're in.

Break out and break free, it cries!

Uranus is also strongly associated with technology. It rules the sign Aquarius, which is, interestingly, the sign that Pluto is now transiting.

How Does Uranus in Gemini Affect You?

Uranus is a planet associated with the air sign Aquarius, and Gemini is also an air sign, so this combo is quite simpatico and lends itself toward inventing brilliant technologies and communicating more directly with each other about how we can make the world a better place.

One caveat is that Uranus moves powerfully toward change, but Gemini can get a little distracted. Therefore, it is most effective for us to set short-term, meetable goals in service to the greater good and our bigger goals. We need to factor in the tendency to be distracted and not expect to stay laser focused on our idealistic goals.

And, yes, Uranus is a planet of idealism. It's also the planet most closely associated with alien life forms, machines, and technology. Add to that Gemini's communication powers and yes, many people do believe we will have contact with extraterrestrials during this cycle. Plenty think we already have, but as we ascend to a higher consciousness that isn't completely attached to our (very limited) five senses, we are at last in a place where we can sense and connect with aliens. Intuitive, empathic people may actually sense the presence of other beings. But with Uranus in chatty, sociable Gemini, you can bet the Internet (or whatever technology succeeds it) will be abuzz with much talk on this subject!

Cue up Radiohead's "Subterranean Homesick Alien" and David Bowie's "Starman," stat!

WHAT SHOULD YOU KNOW ABOUT THE COMBINATION OF URANUS IN GEMINI, NEPTUNE IN ARIES, AND PLUTO IN AQUARIUS?

Astrologers look for patterns and connections, and there's one that is pretty straightforward about this triad of transiting planets. Here we see two air signs (Gemini and Aquarius) and one fire sign (Aries). Signs that share an element are 120 degrees apart in what is called a trine aspect. A trine represents a natural connection, an ease with sharing talents. Air and fire are also compatible. They make a sixty-degree sextile aspect to each other, which represents a sense of cooperation between signs that can lead to great opportunities. In astrology the air and fire signs are deemed masculine, and the earth and water signs feminine. Masculine energy is active and feminine energy is receptive. That means this long cycle is not going to be stagnant! If you think things have been changing at breakneck speed in the twenty-first century, you are correct, but guess what? It's going to get even faster, so buckle up!

STEP TWO

Embody Your Superhero Identity

WELCOME TO THE SUPER-POWERED ZODIAC!

The same twelve signs, each now embodying a superhero identity with a primary power:

THE FACETS OF EACH NEW ZODIAC SUPERHERO

In Step Two of *Super-Powered Astrology* you will learn all about your zodiac superhero alter ego, how to embody this role, what your special superpower is, and how to use it. In addition, you can dig into the ways your sign behaves in love, friendship, and community. You will also learn about your supershadow—the kryptonite you need to be careful of—as well as who your internal superfoes are.

✵ SUPERMYSTICAL KNOWLEDGE ✵

In this section you will also learn about the elegant correspondences between astrology and the tarot. The signs and planets are woven into the tarot in multiple decks and multiple ways. The symbology can inspire you to better assess yourself and your choices in life.

Of the seventy-eight cards in a traditional tarot deck, fifty-six are minor arcana, while only twenty-two are major arcana, also known as trump cards. The minor arcana relate to day-to-day human life, which is often dependent on moods and the micro parts of our lives. The major arcana, however, are connected to universal forces that are powerfully guiding us, trying to help us move in a certain direction.

You will also gain insight into the connection between the zodiac signs and the ancient mystical system of Kabbalah. Part of being a superhero is having access to secret knowledge. When you reach the garden of forking paths in your worldly life, there are questions to consider before making your moves.

Each superhero chapter will also include analysis of the sign's traits by decanate. There are three decanates for each sign. I also use the decanate sections for each sign to discuss upcoming outer planet (Uranus, Neptune, Pluto) transits with more specificity.

You will also discover how Mercury, the planet of communication, behaves through the signs. Learning about your Mercury can help you better connect with the people in your life. It also will show you how to use language to better communicate in the larger world.

Tarot

There are countless tarot decks, but in *Super-Powered Astrology*, I will be referencing the famous Rider-Waite deck.

First published in 1909, the Rider-Waite deck has gone through small variations throughout the years, but its basic symbology remains the same. The writer, Arthur Edward ("A. E.") Waite, born in Brooklyn and raised in London, was a member of the Hermetic Order of the Golden Dawn (an occult organization), an active Freemason and Rosicrucian self-taught scholar, and the author of many texts on Hermetic magic.

The cards were illustrated by Pamela Colman-Smith, a British artist, author, occultist, and suffragist, who was also known as "Pixie." She kept a fanciful circle of friends and was well known for her at-home salon of artists, authors, and occultists. Pixie drew illustrations for Bram Stoker's novel *The Lair of the White Worm* and William Butler Yeats's *Illustrated Verses*. It was Yeats who brought her into the Hermetic Order of the Golden Dawn, which is where she became acquainted with A. E. Waite. And the rest is occult history!

Rabbalah

In each of the twelve chapters on the new zodiac superheroes, I include a little information about how each sign is connected to the symbols of Kabbalah. I also weave in how each sign's major tarot card connects to Kabbalistic wisdom. Kabbalah is an ancient system based on Jewish mysticism. The word *Kabbalah* translates to "receive," the idea being that the hidden mysteries of life are there for us to understand if we open up to receive them.

The basis of this mystical system lies within the Hebrew alphabet, which consists of twenty-two letters (plus a twenty-third "invisible letter"), each of which contains its own primordial meaning. The other key element of Kabbalah is the Tree of Life, which represents the paths we travel on our human journey. The Tree is structured around the ten sefirot—or spheres—that represent divine emanations, and the twenty-two paths that connect the spheres. The astrological signs and cards connect to the Tree of Life with great elegance.

Finally, I offer each sign a magic spell with which to access your powers when you have forgotten you are more than just human. You are a superhero of the infinite!

The Three Decanates

Each sign has three distinct faces, called decanates, determined by birthday. For instance, if you were born in the early part of a sign, you likely exhibit that sign's traits in full force. Whatever planet rules your sign is extra accentuated for first-decanate people.

The mode of that sign (cardinal, fixed, or mutable) is also extra emphasized. Those born in the middle of the Sun sign are influenced by the sign that follows it within its element (fire, earth, air, or water) and the mode of whatever that sign is. Third-decanate people are informed by the sign of the particular element that completes the triad. And that sign's mode will affect these folks strongly too.

For reference see the following:

Elements

Fire Signs: Aries, Leo, Sagittarius (dynamic)

Earth Signs: Taurus, Virgo, Capricorn (grounded)

Air Signs: Gemini, Libra, Aquarius (cerebral)

Water Signs: Cancer, Scorpio, Pisces (emotional)

Modes

Cardinal: Aries, Cancer, Libra, Capricorn (initiators who excel at ideas)

Fixed: Taurus, Leo, Scorpio, Aquarius (stable types who last the long haul)

Mutable: Gemini, Virgo, Sagittarius, Pisces (adaptable, go-with-the-flow types)

Your Mercury Super Sidekick

I think of Mercury almost like a roommate or house pet whom you chat with because they live in such close proximity. Your Mercury is always hanging around and never strays too far.

It engages in *internal* conversation with you constantly. With Uranus transiting Gemini (ruled by Mercury) through 2033 and making a harmonious trine aspect to Pluto in Aquarius, I believe Mercury's influence will be felt more strongly during this period. Mercury is the closest planet to the Sun, and in a natal chart it always falls in the same sign as the Sun or in the sign that precedes or follows it. Check your chart to determine your Mercury position and read about its influence on your Sun sign.

And as for Mercury retrograde, which tends to be a confusing period for communication and technology, I think it is most important to "keep your side of the street clean" and gracefully navigate any small snafus rather than blaming the planet or the universe. But I was born with Mercury retrograde (and still became a writer!), so I tend to look at the whole Merc retro brouhaha somewhat counterintuitively. If you see a capital *R* next to the Mercury symbol in your chart, that indicates you too were born during Mercury retrograde. I think it makes us a little bit luckier than most during those three-week periods. So contrarian!

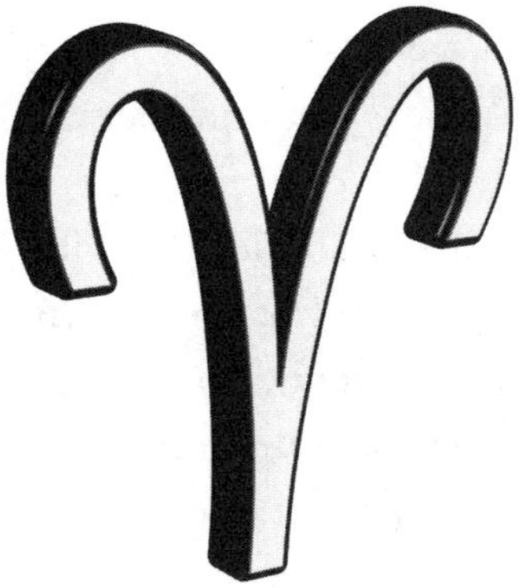

Aries the Warrior

March 21 to April 19

Element: Fire

Mode: Cardinal

Planet: Mars

✵ SUPERPOWER: THE POWER TO ACT ✵

Ruled by Mars, the planet of passion and action, you are a fierce warrior by nature. Known for your bravery and decisiveness, you never wait to see what the herd is doing. Instead, you bolt forward with self-confidence, always excited to play offense, not defense. In previous eras, you might have been called impulsive, but in the wild cycle we are living through, your ability to move forward when others are overthinking is a great gift. Despite your archetype of the Warrior, you don't actually like to go head-on into battle. Your life is full of fun, and you have outlets for your excess energy. Still, if you are dealing with someone who lacks complete integrity, you are not apt to stand passively by. You may not raise your fists, but you could raise your voice.

So what makes a Warrior during these times? For that answer, let's throw it back to fifth century B.C., shall we? That was when Sun Tzu, the Chinese military strategist, wrote in *The Art of War*: "The greatest victory is one which requires no battle." During times of invisibility that we live in—where people can hide behind screens, actual wars can be fought through cyberattacks, and opinions become facts if they go viral—it is easy to not reveal yourself. But you, Aries, are too authentic for that.

You show yourself and you cannot help but be your true self, whether in public or private. This inspires respect. As long as you maintain this level of authenticity, your reputation will precede you and nullify the need to fight. To quote Aries diva Lady Gaga: You were just "born this way." You are a pioneer in your field, just like fellow Aries Charlie Chaplin was to silent movies and Harry Houdini was to magic. You simply don't have it in you to be a follower. So keep running ahead and know that the herd will catch up.

Aries, I want you to take a few deep breaths each morning and tune in to your Warrior ways. Know that you are always brave enough to act when others cower.

SUPERPARTNER POWER

Your honesty, directness, and lack of game and guile make you a wonderful partner. If you like someone, you can't hide it. You just get so excited! The same is true about your feelings in general. Your boo always knows where they stand with you. And they know that if they ask you an important question, you will answer honestly.

You love a challenge and are apt to enjoy a game of run, catch, and kiss. That's when you're courting, as you are competitive and love to win! Once you are involved with someone, you need to keep the action going. You are not one to lie on the couch in your comfortable old slippers. Instead, keeping things physical will keep your ardor up. Yes, that means sex, but physical challenges and activities get you excited too. If your partner can match you with energy, you will be happy.

Your energy, along with your childlike enthusiasm, is also incredibly endearing when focused on your partner. Again, you possess the power to act when others are too timid to. If your partner wants to go out and try someplace new or hang with a new crowd, you are extremely open to changing it up.

SUPERCOMMUNITY POWER

Your pioneering spirit is exciting to be around, and thus those who want a leader often flock to you. You are happy to lead, and you are also fine flying solo. But when your peeps need you, you are there. More often than not, you call a posse together when something important must be done. Whether it's pooling resources for rough times, gathering the creatives together to put on a show, or getting people out on the field or the dance floor, you can handle yourself in a group, especially when you are the ringleader.

And even if you keep to yourself sometimes, you set a great example for others on how to be a peaceful warrior. If you've ever done any Warrior poses in yoga, you know that they summon the power of inner strength and require complete focus and determination. After all, they were named for the mighty Hindu warrior Virabhadra. Talk about street cred.

SUPERSHADOW

Your temper and impatience are the parts of you that live in your shadow, Sun in Aries (and for those with their Moon in Aries, this goes double for you)! It's just so easy for you to go from zero to one hundred. After an explosion you move on quickly, but sometimes the people around you are left shaken. When the dust settles after you get riled up with impatience or lose your cool with a loved one or a colleague, you are likely to feel a little ashamed.

Instead of punishing yourself, try to engage with that red-faced side of yourself. In your mind or in a journal or out loud, have a conversation between your Higher Self and your Angry Self. Something to the effect of:

Higher Self: What's going on?

Angry Self: I don't know why I do that. It's like a bolt of lightning. It hits out of nowhere and I explode with rage. What kind of a person does that?

HS: Well, what else were you feeling in that moment?

AS: Frustration. I don't know why she can't get off the phone when she knows I want to get good seats at the show. And I don't want to hit traffic. But really, what's the big deal? Why did I have to start shouting?

HS: Say more about the frustration. No one likes being disregarded.

AS: No, but it's not like I haven't done the same

thing occasionally. I just felt like, why don't I just f*&king go by myself if she's not excited?

HS: Do you think you would've had a better time without her?

AS: I don't know. When we actually got there everything worked out with seats, but she was giving me the cold shoulder for the way I acted.

HS: Does that remind you of anything from your past?

AS: My mother did that to "teach me a lesson."

HS: That must've been painful.

AS: I realized later it's a form of gaslighting. I mean, at least when I feel something I don't hide it. But then it causes friction in my relationships. It always has. What am I supposed to do?

HS: What about not doing anything? Try to acknowledge what happens and forgive yourself. Don't punish yourself. That only makes it worse. You want to be seen and heard. Maybe if you do that for yourself, you can lower the volume in your head before you need to scream.

You get the idea!

SUPERFOES:

THE DOMINATOR AND THE ME-NO-LISTEN MONSTER

First, the Dominator. As the name implies, the Dominator tends to use force to get what he wants. He steps over people's needs and takes charge too aggressively. He's like that dog in the dog park who has to prove how alpha he is. And unfortunately, the Dominator can't be trained with treats.

Then there is the Me-No-Listen Monster. This krazy kween talks and talks and lacks the ability to reciprocate by giving someone else the floor. This monster is so afraid of not being heard that she doesn't realize she is denying everyone else that very same right!

Sometimes a little humor works best with these folks. The Dominator doesn't like being so vigilant *all the time*. When you find yourself becoming the Dominator, it's best to laugh at yourself. Offering up some humor and warmth can soften up the Dominator a bit and make him into friend, not foe.

If you start to become the MNLM, try rubbing the side of your index finger up and down over the middle of your lips. This comes close to mimicking the "shush" signal, and it's a kind "cue" to give yourself to shut the f&*k up!

MYSTICAL SUPERPOWERS

Tarot

In the tarot, the Emperor signifies a call to action; it is the card that rules Aries. In the classic Rider-Waite tarot deck, he holds the ankh, known in Hermetic circles as "the key of life." His life force is palpable. He sits on his throne but possesses the energy of his ruling planet Mars, ready to spring forth into action. The Emperor can be male, female, nonbinary; the point is that he is in tune with masculine energy. Even in matters of the heart, being assertive is encouraged. And in matters of work and wealth, your mantra should be: "I am the boss of me."

When you are feeling momentarily unsure, practice "breath of fire" as the yogis do or martial arts (if you know what you're doing) to put you in touch with the limitless energy you possess.

Kabbalah

ה

In the ancient mystical system of Kabbalah, Aries is associated with the Emperor, as described above, and the Emperor connects to the fifth primordial letter of the Hebrew alphabet: hei. Hei is a letter of tremendous energy. Rabbi Richard Seidman compares it to the way we say "Hey! Here I am!" and announce our arrival. Hei possesses so much life force, just like you, Aries! When looking at the actual letter, you will see that it contains two distinct pieces: one appears tall, mighty, and elegant, while a smaller piece stands disconnected from the other. Powerful of a force as you may be, Aries, much of your poignant beauty arises when you allow yourself to simply be human. On the Tree of Life your sign travels between Chochmah, the second divine emanation, which represents wisdom, and Tipheret, the sixth sefirot, which translates to "beauty" or "adornment." The sweet spot between these two spheres gives off a distinctly Libra vibe, and Libra is the sign opposite Aries. We all have close relationships with our opposites. And in this case, Libra strives for balance and fairness. When the Emperor prioritizes these qualities, he truly becomes a royal force for good.

You were born during the Hebrew month of Nisan, which is considered the first month of the year on this calendar. This resonates with the way Aries is connected to the first house in the classic Western horoscope template. No wonder. You are a first responder!

Your Magic Spell

When you have forgotten you are more than just human—you are a superhero of the infinite—use this magic spell:

Light a candle, stare into the flame (or use your imagination to do so), and say aloud or silently to yourself:

"I am a Warrior. I take brave action for myself and the world to find the way to freedom.

Universe, what is the most direct and pure path for me to take?"

THE THREE SUPERDECANATES OF ARIES

First-Decanate Aries:

The Mars/Cardinal Decanate

Sun in Aries 0 Degrees to 9 Degrees

Approximately March 20/21 to March 29/30

You early Aries peeps are the most Aries of them all! Your Warrior tendencies shine through in your honorable leadership style. It's not surprising to see you occupying a boss position but not letting the power go to your head. You enjoy being a big brother or sister to those who look up to you, and you enjoy the adulation. But you are not dependent on whether folks adore you or not. You are too focused on your own path to notice how others are receiving you.

Upcoming Outer Planet Transits

Neptune will be transiting Aries through March 23, 2039. The planet of healing and illusion will be making a conjunction to your sign's decanate until April 2029, which could play out in a few ways. You may at times find it hard to use your superpower, the power to act, but during those brief periods, put your energy into meditation and self-care. You are still in training, Aries! Don't ignore the rest and recovery part. You're likely to receive downloads from the universe on the regular. It would behoove you to go to bed at night with a notepad or app by your side so you can ask a question of the universe and see what answers come to you through dreams or direct messages. Pay attention to synchronicity. Your Warrior ways will find a great outlet in the arts, including the healing arts.

Second-Decanate Aries:

The Sun/Fixed Decanate

Sun in Aries 10 Degrees to 19 Degrees

Approximately March 30/31 to April 8/9

The Sun fills you with energy, like your fellow fire sign, Leo. And this solar influence also adds to your innate optimism. Your upbeat attitude plays out very strongly in your love life. You believe in soulmates and often have a stronger romantic streak than other Aries people. You enjoy playing the conquering hero, but your huge heart is your greatest weapon.

Upcoming Outer Planet Transits

Thanks to Pluto's influence, between February 2029 and March 2037, you may feel a little bit of opposition from the universe if you take a "my way or the highway" stance. So please don't! Instead, think about your goal and work backwards. Use your strategic powers to get you to where you are going and make sure to nurture your key relationships along the way.

Third-Decanate Aries:

The Jupiter/Sagittarius Decanate

Sun in Aries 20 Degrees to 29 Degrees

Approximately April 10/11 to April 19/20

Of all the Aries people, you are apt to be the most lucky duck! Jupiter, after all, is the planet of good fortune, and it's also the most fun! You have a lighter vibe than your fellow Aries peeps. You are also more adaptable, thanks to the mutable influence of Jupiter's sign: Sagittarius. You are also most likely to be a visionary or to be obsessed with teaching, learning, and discovering the meaning of life. Yes, you can be fanatical, but you also can laugh at yourself, Guru!

Upcoming Outer Planet Transits

Uranus will be stirring up your communication talents from May 2030 to late May 2033 in the mutable sign of the Messenger: Gemini. The more you focus on your own particular message the better. Focus on themes that are of mega importance to you during this cycle. You have the power to influence hearts and minds with your words. This may also be a period in which you want to access as much information as you can, and research and network like a banshee too. You have the ability to synthesize knowledge and then translate it to the greater world.

❋ YOUR MERCURY SUPER SIDEKICK ❋

Aries Sun with Mercury in Aries: You say what you mean and mean what you say. Mercury in Aries makes you double down on cutting to the chase. Although you are always in a hurry, your excitement can be contagious and gets others to shake a leg too.

Aries Sun with Mercury in Pisces: Mercury in Pisces Aries people are a little softer around the edges and speak with more empathy and gentleness. Like Pisces, you are very intuitive, and sometimes when you put your thoughts into words you show a strong psychic/predictive streak. You folks are also extra imaginative and creative.

Aries Sun with Mercury in Taurus: The Taurus influence on you makes you more willing to stick to projects and people for a long stretch of time. You likely have a little more patience and sense of decorum than the typical Aries. You may also have a lovely speaking and singing voice.

Taurus the Maker

April 20 to May 20

Element: Earth

Mode: Fixed

Planet: Venus

SUPERPOWER: THE POWER TO BUILD

As an earth sign, Taurus, you are most at home when you can touch things with your hands and create something material where before there was nothing. Your superhero identity is the Maker, who possesses the power to build. Even if you work a job that is all virtual, the time you spend in your real life needs to be in the physical realm. Whether your hands are covered with soil in the garden, flour in the kitchen, clay in the studio, or paint outside the barn, you are the most embodied and physical of all the zodiac signs.

Building doesn't just have to mean making things with your hands, though. Taurus's ruling planet is artistic, romantic Venus. Each sign also rules an area of the body. For you that is your neck and throat. It's no wonder then that you folks also are gifted with a strong talent for and connection to music. Even though you have a reputation for being stubborn, I would describe you as "stable." Many of you Taureans are especially musically gifted, whether you possess the gift of playing music or singing, or you just have great taste in music. Taureans seem to possess the ability to tune in to the frequency of any art and connect to it in a way that makes it feel even more real and human.

Taurus the Maker, there is one more thing that you especially love to make: MONEY! Famous Taureans include piano man Billy Joel, velvet-voiced Barbra Streisand, timeless icon George Clooney, and Spanish artist Salvador Dali. You folks like to save up and build a nest egg. And although you are tactile and appreciate luxury, you still often have "your mind on your money and your money on your mind" (to paraphrase Snoop Dogg). It's an ability to understand how the real world works that allows you to take great care of yourself and your loved ones by creating material stability. In a world of chaos, this is no small feat!

Remember, Taurus, you can build whatever you set your mind to—whether it's building bridges between friends and creating community, building a savings account to provide comfort for later years, or slowly building the foundation for the life you've always wanted. Or all of the above.

✵ SUPERPARTNER POWER ✵

You are a lover, not a fighter. Taureans are well suited to enjoy sweet, calm romantic relationships. Your partner loves you because you are always *there*. Running around and disappearing is just not your style. Rather, being on time for your honey's homemade dinner at six or preparing dinner for you both (which may frequently include potatoes) is how you play. Not a fan of surprises, you make a great partner because of your consistency and reliability. If this sounds dull to some, then let them go. For those who dig your vibe, they will be pleasantly surprised by your smoldering sensuality in the sack. Again, you have Venus as your ruler, and you are most at home with a partner on your own.

Your superpower, of course, is the power to build, and this goes double for relationships. Commitment is your forte, and marriage suits your steady, patient nature. You make a great partner because of your strength of character and your ability to run the show in a quiet way. Paying bills, finding the best real estate, and making a house feel like home for your person and your children or furbabies comes naturally.

Leaving a relationship is really, really hard for you. Even when there are troubles, you would almost always choose to weather them rather than endure the upheaval of a breakup. Being this risk-averse can be problematic at times, though. Working on a relationship will always require open communication, and you may be too afraid to rock the boat to say what you really think. Shutting down, crossing your arms across your chest, and digging in rather than adapting to change is where you can get into trouble.

Luckily, your instinct to choose a partner wisely can help you avoid these pitfalls. A happy home is of utmost importance to you. Happy wife, happy life. (Or, to be more inclusive: Happy honey, lotsa money, life is sunny!)

SUPERCOMMUNITY POWER

The flavor of the month is of no interest to you when it comes to your homies. Tried and true is how you roll. People trust you because you are a straight shooter, true to your word, and you don't have a hidden agenda. In terms of larger community, your archetype of the Builder allows you to offer useful contributions to group endeavors. First off, you are able to keep things simple. One or two good ideas is often all you need to make good intentions turn into an actual service to the community. While others can sometimes overload the process with free-associative tangents and wild gimmicks, you actually know how to build a system that adds value.

You can blend homebody and activist quite smoothly as you serve up guac and chips at your house and supply folks with posterboard and markers to make protest signs. (And if no one shows, guess what? More guac and chips for you!) But truly: Cooking and hosting or simply providing a safe space for the crew makes you indispensable. You can also shine with your smarts around financial matters. If money needs to be raised for charity, you know where to start and how to monetize the goodwill of the people. In essence, you are a pro at *showing up* and at offering practical solutions to problems stumping the group.

SUPERSHADOW

Ruled by harmonious, loving Venus, you can be easygoing, and nondemanding. As long as you have your favorite cozy spot and some comfort food, you are practically a saint. The shadow side of you tries to control your environment and the earthy parts of life to an almost obsessive degree. You present as laid-back, and generally you are, but in your quiet way you may sometimes find yourself unable to deal with having to replace furniture or meet a friend for lunch at 12:30 instead of 12:45.

This is the kind of stuff that sounds endearing to a degree, but relationships are built on the cumulative effect of thousands of tiny decisions and behaviors. With that in mind, it would be wise for you to treat this part of you like your inner child (which she is) and uncover what she is afraid of. It could be that your nervous system is so used to running a specific program of sorts that it shuts down when there is an update or an unexpected glitch. Just make sure you are kind to the little kid in you who needs comfort and routine in a deeply profound way. Once that kid feels heard and safe, she likely will be able to (slowly) learn to adapt.

SUPERFOES:
THE STICK IN THE MUD MONSTER AND SLOTH-A-TAURUS

There are monsters who shriek and attack, and monsters who hide and feed on their host like a virus. Guess which kind your superfoes are, Taurus?

The Stick in the Mud Monster is the Debbie Downer that acts like a buzzkill in any social setting. If loved ones or colleagues are having a good time and the Stick in the Mud wants to leave, he will make sure he destroys the good vibes before he exits. He might insist on splitting the check exactly before dessert and nickel-and-dime everyone not just out of a few extra bucks but out of a much more precious commodity: good times!

And if you think this cat is a bummer, wait until you meet Sloth-a-Taurus. So lazy is this creature that it will not take a shower if guests are coming if it "doesn't feel like it." Sloth-a-Taurus is most known for moving so slowly that even the most high-tech motion sensors report "no movement." And forget about it if he's in a slow-talking mood. He will blather on in a sleep-inducing monotone, sharing boring details by the bushel, and never *ever* get to the point. When interrupted, he suddenly loses his sense of hearing. If anyone tries to rush him, he doubles down on his slothiness. Brave souls have been lured in by his cuteness, only to be bored to death—literally!

Just remember to be direct but *gentle* when calling out your superfoes. They don't realize the impact of their ways. So preface any critique with "I know you're not doing this on purpose, but . . ."

✵ MYSTICAL SUPERPOWERS ✵

Tarot

In the Rider-Waite tarot deck, Taurus corresponds to the fifth trump card, the Hierophant, which is sometimes known as the High Priest. The illustration shows a pope-like figure sitting on a throne. His goal is to take the meaningful essence of spirituality and bring it down to earth for the people. In the center of his cloak, a white strip of fabric holds the two sides together.

For you, Taurus the Maker, this card symbolizes your superpower: the power to build. In fact, the name of this card translates to "bridge builder." In this case, what you are building is a bridge between heaven and earth. Think about the Hermetic maxim "as above, so below" and apply it to your day-to-day life.

Rabbalah

ו

Taurus corresponds with the sixth primordial letter of the Hebrew alphabet, vav, which is associated with connection. In the Tree of Life, you are connected to the path that links Chokmah (wisdom) and Chesed (mercy). Both these spheres unite in a certain gentleness of spirit, Taurus, a gentility you embody. Ruled by Venus, you prefer calm over chaos. Therefore, if you see someone less mature than you who has not yet gained your worldly wisdom, you are merciful enough to teach them better. You connect to a soul who is still learning with kind benevolence.

In Kabbalah, the month associated with Taurus is Iyar. This second month on the Hebrew calendar is associated with the sixth letter, vav, as described above, as well as the sixteenth letter, pei, which is associated with Taurus's ruler, Venus. *Pei* translates to "mouth" and is a great reminder of how we should practice the habit of "right speech." Taureans are generally known to be people of few words but whose words mean something.

Your Magic Spell

When you have forgotten you are more than just human—you are a superhero of the infinite—use this magic spell:

Put your hand in the soil (or use your imagination to do so) and say aloud or silently to yourself:

"I am a Maker. I build stable creations that make the world more beautiful and secure.
Universe, what is the most solid path for me to take?"

THE THREE SUPERDECANATES OF TAURUS

First-Decanate Taurus:
The Venus/Fixed Decanate

Sun in Taurus 0 Degrees to 9 Degrees

Approximately April 20 to April 29

First-decanate Tauruses double down on their superpowers. These early Taureans love to make things with their hands and create beautiful sounds with their voices. They love food and real estate, and especially money! The other side of early-decanate

Tauruses is that money is *such* a hot-button issue. If you were born during this decanate, take the time to analyze your ingrained beliefs about money and help yourself let go of or transform the counterproductive beliefs. For example, rather than putting off big purchases like a house or well-made car out of an overdeveloped sense of caution, reframe them as investments.

Remember, a belief is not based on empirical evidence. Rather, it is something that is repeated again and again until we are convinced it is true.

Upcoming Outer Planet Transits

Transiting Pluto in Aquarius, will be making a square aspect to your Sun in early Taurus through February 2031. Square aspects tend to emphasize conflicts based on stubbornness. Neither side wants to give an inch. The Aquarian tendency to make sudden changes could conflict with the Taurean desire to leave well enough alone. What would the wisest version of yourself, known as your Higher Self, do if she was put in charge of mediating this conflict? You can discover the answers though meditating with the intention of receiving wisdom, or journaling in question and answer form. What questions would she ask you? What guidance would she suggest in navigating your relationship with Pluto? You may be set in your ways, but you also have tremendous wisdom and maturity. I have faith in you to make the necessary changes you need to make in the New World. And rest assured, you can do them incrementally, in baby steps, *baby*!

Second-Decanate Taurus:

The Mercury/Mutable Decanate

Sun in Taurus 10 Degrees to 19 Degrees

Approximately April 30 to May 9

Because of the effect of Mercury, the ruler of fellow earth sign Virgo, you middle Taureans are incredibly process-oriented. Whereas many Taureans are black-and-white thinkers and apt to say yes or no, rarely maybe, *you* really like to get into the weeds and figure out the inner workings of a system. With the influence of a mutable sign on your naturally fixed nature, you are also more adaptable than your average Taurus. Think about what you want to build in your life and be open to tweaking your process so that when the world changes you don't just stay stuck in an old way of doing business.

Upcoming Outer Planet Transits

Pluto, the planet of self-transformation, will be making a square aspect to your Sun in middle Taurus from February 2029 through February 2037. This can be a little challenging if you take the inflexible path. Given that you have the mutable influence of Mercury as part of your decanate, you should do well. But you are still a change-fearing Taurus, so here's a little advice on how to navigate your moments of worry: Writing in your journal or having a conversation out loud with yourself can really help you put your fears into words. The Mercury influence on your Sun adds to your ability to use logic to get through occasional anxiety.

Third-Decanate Taurus:

The Saturn/Cardinal Decanate

Sun in Taurus 20 Degrees to 29 Degrees

Approximately May 10 to May 20/21

The influence of serious Saturn likely made you feel wise beyond your years as a child. Perhaps you had a streak of melancholy. This may add to an overly realistic and pessimistic outlook on life. You simply absorbed a lot from the adult world, in all its toughness, at way too young an age. The good news is that the influence of Saturn also ensures that you will feel younger the older you get. You age beautifully on a physical level, and with each passing year you learn how to give much fewer f*cks what other people think.

Late Taurus people are the kind of Makers who build things that are meant to last. You earn respect easily by really putting effort into craftsmanship, whether you are building a relationship, a work of art, or an investment portfolio.

Upcoming Outer Planet Transits

Pluto, the planet of self-transformation, in the future-oriented sign Aquarius will be making a square aspect to your Sun in late Taurus from June 2030 through late June 2033. Pluto will want you to use technology, learn new skills, and adapt to a world that is changing at a rapid pace. Use your mind like a young and passionate inventor.

✵ YOUR MERCURY SUPER SIDEKICK ✵

Taurus Sun with Mercury in Taurus: Of all the Taureans you are the most straightforward communicator. Your demeanor and tone tend to make everyone feel comfortable. We are all animals, aren't we? And we respond to tone more than words. Ruled by Venus, you possess an artful way of communicating your message.

Taurus Sun with Mercury in Aries: Taurus people with Mercury in Aries are quicker to form an opinion and to speak than other Taureans. Aries is the sign of impulse and possesses a strong urge to act. Just be conscious of reading the room correctly and not overwhelming others with your strong will and fierce certainty.

Taurus Sun with Mercury in Gemini: Mercury rules Gemini, so this is considered an exalted placement, meaning it operates at maximum capacity. You take the Taurus's usual slow way of approaching life and speed it up a little, at least intellectually. These Taureans are often people who love going out with friends and brainstorming about whatever's new and fascinating.

Gemini the Messenger

May 21 to June 21

Element: Air

Mode: Mutable

Planet: Mercury

SUPERPOWER: THE POWER TO COMMUNICATE

Gemini, your mind races with brilliant as well as shallow thoughts. You absorb news, gossip, art, politics, sports, business, fashion, and every subject under the sun, and several from other planets, and manage to mix them up in your high-speed Cuisinart of a brain. You have a way with words, nimble social skills, and innate curiosity. So what do you need? Focus!

You are the Messenger, after all, and in this era of constant change it's up to you to find the one simple, clear message that resonates for you and make it your calling card. For example, let's say technology is your obsession, something you've been excited by since you were a kid. Rather than just read up on what company is releasing which device 3.0 or software 7.0 and then becoming a master at using these technologies, try a more macro approach. Think about how these individual advances connect to the needs of the larger world. For instance, maybe they both have a shared purpose of making communication in different languages similar. Use the connections you notice to ask yourself bigger questions like "What would it take to create a simple unified language that is used around the globe?"

This does not mean you need to have one singular message from the time you turn eighteen until your ninety-eighth birthday. The world keeps changing, and you, being a mutable sign, possess the gift of adaptability. Yet, even if you focus on a variety of messages you feel compelled to communicate throughout your life, I would bet there is still one overarching message that serves as an umbrella under which all the others fall.

Think of inspiring fellow Geminis like Rachel Carson, marine biologist and author of *Silent Spring* (the 1962 book that many say kick-started the environmental movement), and a host of musician/songwriters, each with their own unique style and message, such as Bob Dylan, Lauryn Hill, Kendrick Lamar, Paul McCartney, Stevie Nicks, and Prince. Your life should be more like a concept album, rather than a greatest hits collection, with one bold, clear theme connecting all the tracks.

You are the Messenger, Gemini. And at your best, you can convey wisdom from the universe in your everyday dealings, as well as larger work in the world. Remember, your superpower is the ability to communicate. You have the ability to ascertain the essence of what your fellow humans are trying to share. And you are quick and adept at finding the common thread that makes people feel connection, not suspicion.

✵ SUPERPARTNER POWER ✵

Getting your attention for more than three minutes can be a challenge, so you may tend toward periods in your life that are full-on date-a-thons with no commitment or intimacy. You love to have a best friend with benefits for spontaneous, hot quickies followed by tons of chitchat and random binge-watching of your favorite show. And you can get so used to this type of fun that you will eventually want to go all in. Your partner just needs to know that you also require plenty of alone time to just stare at an invisible spot on the wall, like a house cat.

You sometimes freak yourself out, worrying that you will be bored if you settle down. The idea of being in a particular routine and schedule for life may make you ill, but you do like short bursts of routine, like preparing for a triathlon, going sugar-free for six weeks, or doing a Swedish language immersion class. (Skål!) And for these kinds of routines you adore sharing the excitement and short-term commitment with a partner, whether romantic or platonic. You have the power to infuse joy into a partnership with your infectious enthusiasm.

✵ SUPERCOMMUNITY POWER ✵

Your brain never shuts off, nor does your body—except when you completely crash. It is just this kind of energy that makes you a gift to your friend group and community. Even though you are perfectly happy to sit on the porch with an iced tea doing *The New York Times* crossword puzzle, you still can't resist a last-minute invite to do something fun and frivolous like ziplining or performing improv theater. So much of what your peeps get from you is the message "lighten up." You never make your serious friends feel bad about their intensity, but you certainly lead by example when you ditch a dull meeting and instead make it a roller-skating afternoon followed by a chatty mani-pedi.

When times are tough and your community really needs you, you know how to show up. Your style is to arrive in short bursts, suggest great ideas, follow through with teamwork, and then get everybody to go out for beers. And of course, since your superpower is communication, you are able to fine-tune the messaging your crew needs.

SUPERSHADOW

Endearing and fun as you can be, your shadow side can be quite chilly, and you may shut down if someone tries to get beyond your walls. You have practiced the art of sharing and opening up, which comes easily to you thanks to your super communication power. But then there's that point when those close to you would like to go a little deeper. What are you passionate about? What are you truly afraid of? You get annoyed when emotionally clingy people try to become truly intimate with you. But can it be that every lover you've ever had, every close friend or sibling or parent has been too clingy? Or are *you* the common denominator, the one who doesn't like to go to deep? That's your prerogative. But then ask yourself: What do you get out of relationships with people who are more feelings-oriented? Perhaps you too get bored if you are around people who close down as easily as you do. Maybe you actually enjoy when your friends go deep since you sometimes avoid the depths. Do some self-inquiry and don't let yourself off the hook so easily, Gemini!

✵ SUPERFOES ✵

THE COLD BEEYATCH AND THE SO-BORED-YOU'RE-BORING MONSTER

Gemini, you may go to sleep at night after a day spent charming the masses with witty comebacks and clever ideas. But you could wake up in the morning a different creature: the Cold Beeyatch. This scary beast is a terror to anyone who wants to experience authentic connection. Maybe your coworker asks you about your weekend, and you take the opportunity to snidely mock his lack of social life. Why? Maybe you were blown off by someone you like, and instead of processing your own feelings of rejection or telling the truth about it, you get sharp. And I don't mean funny sharp. I mean nasty sharp.

The other superfoe you occasionally embody is guilty of something that makes you cringe: being tedious. This foe is just so bored by everything and everyone that he misses the obvious: He's the boring one! In general, you Geminis are good at entertaining yourselves. But secretly, you know you can be dependent on other people. You just love getting a reaction. And it's not always enough to get reactions from just anyone; sometimes it feels the best when it's from someone you think is cooler, smarter, or more talented than you are. And when someone like that focuses on what they are interested in and seems bored by your superficial chatter, you freak out. You would never show your vulnerable emotions, so you turn into the So-Bored-You're-Boring-Monster, who yawns and eye-rolls his way through the day. This act is getting old, and it's time to retire it!

When you find yourself turning into either of these superfoes, try a little trick to snap yourself out of it. Place your hand over your heart for a moment and remind yourself that you don't need to hide from your feelings. Whether it's the fear of intimacy or a fear of not being cool enough, this is your cue to reassure yourself that you are enough.

✵ MYSTICAL SUPERPOWERS ✵

Tarot

The sixth major arcana card, the Lovers, is ruled by your sign, Gemini. In the classic Rider-Waite tarot deck, it is illustrated with a dreamy-looking nude couple presided over by a benevolent angel. Tarot scholars Johannes Fiebig and Evelin Burger interpret the card as an imagining of what Adam and Eve felt like when they *returned* to paradise. They probably had a lot to talk about!

The Lovers card symbolizes romantic love, yes, but it is also associated with finding harmony in one's life. Something to consider is how much you love yourself. The person who comes into your life as a partner can serve as a mirror. And just as we can't change the image in a mirror, only change ourselves, it serves as a reminder to be the best version of yourself. That includes treating yourself with care and respect.

Kabbalah

ז

In ancient mystical Kabbalah, Gemini is associated with the seventh Hebrew letter, zayin, which possesses the primordial energy of discrimination. *Zayin* translates to "sword." The sword's meaning is paradoxical. It can be an instrument of war, but it can also keep the peace. Gemini the Messenger, who possesses the power to communicate, has the ability to use words as weapons or as instruments of peace.

On the Tree of Life, Gemini travels the path between the third sphere, Binah (understanding), and the sixth sephirot, Tiphareth (beauty). The understanding of Binah can only come through solitary contemplation. When we calm our minds in the stillness of meditation, we can detach from the egoic "I" and see with the observer "eye." When we can see ourselves, others, and the world with this kind of compassionate clarity, we can experience true beauty in the form of love and art. We can see the beauty in everything.

Gemini is connected to the Hebrew month of Sivan, the time in which we receive divine instruction. Gemini, who possesses a superpower in the form of communication, is tasked with this gift and burden: to learn and to teach by creating a balance between the universal mind and the singular fractal of a human mind.

Your Magic Spell

When you have forgotten you are more than just human—you are a superhero of the infinite—use this magic spell:

Wave your arms over your head three times and feel the air move between your hands (or use your imagination to do so), and say aloud or silently to yourself:

"I am a Messenger. I communicate directions from universal intelligence to help myself and the world to understand our mission.

Universe, what is the clearest path for me to take?"

THE THREE SUPERDECANATES OF GEMINI

First-Decanate Gemini:

The Mercury/Mutable Decanate

Sun in Gemini 0 Degrees to 9 Degrees

Approximately May 20/21 to May 30

You early Geminis are lightning quick in your thoughts and actions. You may change your mind mid-sentence, not out of fickleness but because another dimension or layer to an idea has revealed itself to you. You use words as tools of seduction, making you a conversational pied piper. You have double the influence of Mercury, and combined with your extramutable mode, you do tend to be rather changeable. But this is a gift in your case, as you know how to adapt. We live in times of great upheaval and ideological fighting. You manage to keep a detached eye on what is going on in the world, and you have the ability to breathe through conflict and approach the mad goings-on with a healthy amount of curiosity and openness. You truly want to learn.

Upcoming Outer Planet Transits

Uranus is transiting your Sun until July 2028, infusing you with all sorts of new ideas and ideals, with a strong dose of twenty-first-century technology thrown in. This transit may find you swimming happily in a think tank! As the Messenger, you should ponder what is the message you want to put out to the world, whether in words or perhaps through symbol, logo, or sound frequency. The more you pare down your communication, the better. Less is more, even if you have to brainstorm and revise your ideas over and over again. You'll still find great joy in doing work that involves communication and creation. In personal matters, move toward people who are multilingual and like to travel and discover other cultures.

Second-Decanate Gemini:

The Venus/Cardinal Decanate

Sun in Gemini 10 Degrees to 19 Degrees

Approximately May 30 to June 10

You middle-decanate Geminis have more of a romantic and artistic bent than your Gemini brethren. The influence of Venus makes you very keen to find and experience aesthetic beauty and true love. You are a lover, not a fighter, and may argue less than your typical Messenger. Your superpower of communication is often used in a more intimate way. You believe if you can connect deeply with your person, you can then lead a peaceful, meaningful life. The cardinal aspect of this decanate brings a strong form of initiative and an ability to start projects and make bold choices. You enjoy creating and working with others.

Upcoming Outer Planet Transits

Pluto, the planet of self-transformation, is transiting Aquarius and will be making a trine aspect to your Sun from January 2029 to mid-March 2037. This cycle is quite favored, as Aquarius will be making a smooth and harmonious trine to your Sun. Whatever change the world goes through, you are apt to be in just the right place at the right time. This is a period that is very influenced by the romantic, artistic planet Venus. You may have to actively choose love over war on a daily basis, the way a pianist sits at the keyboard for hours a day. You are paying homage to the concept of peace with every little thing you do in your personal as well as professional life.

Third-Decanate Gemini:

The Uranus/Fixed Decanate

Sun in Gemini 20 Degrees to 29 Degrees

Approximately June 10/11 to June 21/22

Late-decanate Gemini, you are the most intellectually extreme of the bunch. With the futuristic planet Uranus affecting you so strongly, you simply don't see the logic in living in the past. And since each present moment leads us to each future moment, you are always looking ahead. The bigger picture of how the world works and what humanity's role in it should be are subjects that fascinate and drive you. You are so smart that you probably intimidate many with your intelligence. The ones that matter are the ones who are part-genius, just like you. The fixed element of your decanate makes you more stubborn, and despite your open-mindedness, you do tend to chart a decisive course for yourself and resist changing directions.

Upcoming Outer Planet Transits

Uranus will be transiting your Sun in Gemini from mid-August 2029 until late May 2033. Uranus is ready to create a new and better world, and invent technologies and humane systems that allow us to become an advanced civilization in which all are treated with respect. It's a big leap, but keep your ideals high because you can be part of the miracle. During this cycle, think more about what the collective needs rather than focusing on blind ambition. Your superpower of communication is going to be necessary to lighten the vibe between conflicting forces. With massive changes likely in the world at large, you can be the one who mediates between those who want to create radically new paradigms and those who want to hang on to the past.

Gemini Sun with Mercury in Gemini: Mercury rules your sign, Gemini, so those of you with this combination are blessed with an extra gift of communication skills. Take advantage by immersing yourself in foreign languages so you can be the citizen of the world you were born to be.

Gemini Sun with Mercury in Taurus: Taurus is ruled by lovely Venus and associated with the throat and throat chakra. This position tends to add a beautiful voice to your many charms. Try something as an experiment: Speak more slowly. The influence of Mercury in Taurus could help you let go of Gemini's nervous energy and really think through your thoughts instead of just spouting them out.

Gemini Sun with Mercury in Cancer: The Cancer energy infuses your speech and your writing with more emotion than the average Gemini. You emanate soul, and you are connected to the moods of others, making you a very sensitive Gemini.

Cancer the Guardian

June 22 to July 22

Element: Water

Mode: Cardinal

Planet: Moon

SUPERPOWER: THE POWER TO PROTECT

As a water sign, you are ruled by your heart and emotions. It doesn't matter what someone says; you tune in to how you feel around them. Similarly, your intuition is strong, and even when the herd wants to go back, you may continue to climb if that's what your instincts dictate. Of course, you need a good detachment practice to keep your feelings from overwhelming you. Whether you meditate, play soccer, or stare at a painting for an hour, you definitely benefit from detaching from the oceanic waves of emotion that sometimes threaten to drown you.

Cancer, you have a nobility about you when it comes to nurturing the people in your life and all the things that matter—whether it's your family, your home, your business, or nature itself. You recognize what is truly valuable, and you honor it. The more vulnerable the person or thing you are caring for, the more avidly you protect it. We live in a disposable world, but you have created a line in the sand and refuse to succumb to this cynical paradigm.

The depth of your nurturing takes so many forms, you want to make sure to have an outlet for when you feel overwhelmed. Lana Del Rey, Cancerian singer/songwriter/goddess, weaves myriad moods and tales in her songs, and she gives listeners a way in to connect to their own confused and confusing hearts. Cancerian actor Jacob Elordi can embody a noble beast like Frankenstein's monster, who anonymously performs acts of kindness and shows innocence and openness before he is turned upon by the villagers.

Or maybe you can take inspiration from fierce activist Malala Yousafzai, who has spent a lifetime fighting for women's and children's rights. Or George Orwell, who spoke truth to power and tried to protect we humans of the future. You Cancers care, and you care deeply.

SUPERPARTNER POWER

Home is where your heart is, so anyone who wants to get with you must have a domesticated nature. But that doesn't mean you aren't an animal when you are in the mood! It just means that having a solid home base and a sense of permanence works for you. The consistency of partnership is of great importance to you. And let's face it, you do best with a partner who is a good cook (and/or loves your cooking) and is a bit of a mind reader.

Every couple of days, when the Moon changes signs, so does your mood! You may have days when you have the dynamic grace and focus of a tightrope walker, other days when you prefer to reside in a hermetic cave, others when you want to bang shots with the gang, and on and on. Luckily, if you and your partner keep calendars noting the ups, downs, and in-betweens, you will both understand the method to your madness and the consistency of your cycle. If it sounds like I am calling you high-maintenance . . . well, just a little bit, sometimes.

But what you offer is above and beyond what any lover could ask for. Whether you are male, female, or a blend of genders, you have a deeply nurturing nature and innately understand how to be a mother and a father, depending on your loved one's needs. What your love may not have received from their own parents you may very well fill in. And you have a strange way of making all this not just sweet but damn sexy. You may do both tender and top, butch and bottom; just as many variations and costumes as you have moods.

SUPERCOMMUNITY POWER

Cancer the Guardian, you are an absolute asset to your community and to your band of buddies. Since you possess the power to protect, you feel right at home making sure your neighbors, your friends, and any groups you are aligned with feel you guarding over them. Cancer is a cardinal sign, and cardinals in astrology are the leaders, the initiators.

If your friend group is starting to fracture because of the

demands of adult life and the chaos of conflicting schedules, you will likely be the one to arrange a potluck or poker night at your crib. You are the one who understands best what unifies a group and makes them cohere into a family unit of sorts. You are often the glue holding it all together, so don't forget to delegate duties sometimes. *Rhonda, you bring the taco fixin's this time!*

SUPERSHADOW

You are so deeply trustworthy, and you really love to tend to those you love—or even just like—with an open heart. You make people feel good about themselves, and you are thoughtful and kind. But if you have a difficult period with a friend or loved one, you may have a habit of saying to yourself, "I'll never trust them again." Obviously, this can be rough on the people around you, but it really is hardest on you. After all, if it were as simple as recognizing that someone is untrustworthy, lacking in integrity, etc., you could simply tell yourself you dodged a bullet and move on. The problem is that you keep brooding over the fight, misunderstanding, whatever the issue, and you end up giving this person a lot of real estate in your head.

Luckily, one of your greatest gifts is your sense of humor, so perhaps there is a part of you that can remember the feeling you had when laughing with whomever the person on your sh*t list is. The frequency of laughter cannot be held at the same time as anger, and it might just remind you of the good times and allow you to open up again. If it's not meant to be, fine, but remember, the only way to let go is to take responsibility for your part in the fracture.

❋ SUPERFOES ❋

THE GUILT GHOUL AND THE RESENTMENT MONSTER

Regardless of your religious affiliation, you get a secret kick out of guilting people. You're a Guilt Ghoul! This is likely because you put yourself through so much inner criticism and carry around a lot of guilt and shame—which you shouldn't! You are a person of great heart and integrity. Still, old habits are hard to break. Try forgiving yourself more often; this will make you much less apt to sit in the dark next time a loved one accidentally turns the light off.

The Resentment Monster might be even more dangerous. Sometimes we can all laugh a little at the Guilt Ghoul, but the Resentment Monster walks around pissed the f*ck off! This monster holds grudges and resents people who "have it easy." Try this: Draw a picture of your Resentment Monster. Make it furry and funny and threatening but also cute. Again, you have a great sense of humor, so use it before the monster turns on you!

❋ MYSTICAL SUPERPOWERS ❋

Tarot

In the classic Rider-Waite tarot deck, the major arcana card associated with Cancer is the Chariot, the seventh of the twenty-two trumps in the deck. The Chariot suggests that you are master of your own destiny. You are the charioteer, which means you hold the reins. That being the case, you must know your destination, your goal or ambition, and what your deeper motivation is. This card always reminds me of the Steven Spielberg World War II film, *Saving Private Ryan*. In it, Captain John Miller, played by Tom Hanks (a Cancer!) is charged with leading his troops in search of a missing soldier. Private Ryan's family has already lost several sons, and the soldiers are tasked with locating Ryan in Normandy, France, and bringing him home alive to his family in the United States (the U.S. is also a Cancer!) As the mission grows more grueling, Miller explains to his men that he doesn't really give a damn about Private Ryan; he just wants to find Ryan so that he can go home to *his* family.

With this in mind, you Cancerians can learn something from the Chariot card by questioning what your definition of *home* is and what you need to do to return there. You may find this query mystifying, but be patient. The sphinxes, representative of life's mysteries, sit in front of the Chariot as a reminder that silent time with oneself can reveal all.

Kabbalah

ח

In the ancient mystical system of Kabbalah, the sign Cancer is associated with the eighth primordial letter of the Hebrew alphabet, chet. Chet is connected to a symbolic gateway. When you are ready to rise up to a higher frequency, chet is there to help you.

On the Tree of Life, Cancer is associated with the eighth path, the one that connects the third sephirot, Binah, and the fifth sephirot, Gevurah. Binah represents understanding; Gevurah, strength and discipline. It is a bridge that connects kindness and thoughtfulness with the will to manifest in the physical world.

The month associated with Cancer is Tammuz, ruled by your planet, the Moon. The Hebrew calendar is deeply linked to lunar cycles, as are you, Cancer. Tammuz is considered the month of healing. It is quite fitting for someone like you, who is so adept at caring for and nurturing others.

Your Magic Spell

When you have forgotten you are more than just human—you are a superhero of the infinite—use this magic spell:

Put your fingertips in water and gently touch your heart (or use your imagination to do so), and say aloud or silently to yourself:

"I am a Guardian. I protect myself and the world by sheltering all that is good and keeping it safe.
Universe, what is the most direct and pure path for me to take?"

THE THREE SUPERDECANATES OF CANCER

First-Decanate Cancer:
The Lunar/Cardinal Decanate

Sun in Cancer 0 Degrees to 9 Degrees

Approximately June 21/22 to July 3

As an early-decanate Cancer, you tend to be the most moony of the bunch! By that I mean that you are preternaturally tuned in to the lunar cycles, so if you don't follow them on your calendar, you should! Your moods are powerful, and so are your culinary and decorating skills! You have an extra helping of Cancer influencing you, so naturally you put energy into making your home welcoming. Spending time near the water is good for your soul, as is any time in nature with your hands in the earth. Allow the athlete in you to come out, as sweating out the toxins also helps you sweat out any bad mood. You likely will come off the field feeling quite jolly. Routines suit you well, as does a calm living environment. I pray that you never have to ask, "Who moved my cheese?!"

Upcoming Outer Planet Transits

Through February 2031, Neptune, the planet of healing and illusion, will be transiting the early degrees of Aries and squaring your Sun in Cancer. Squares are an aspect meant to teach us the art of compromise. Often there will be forces beyond our control and people "in our way" that make forging ahead with plans feel thwarted. However, the lesson here is to let go of previous expectations and deal with "what is." Accept the reality of the now, and the traffic jams and bickering come to an end. Once you become comfortable with how things *are* instead of griping over how you expect them to be, you actually can manifest what you desire up the wazoo!

Second-Decanate Cancer:
The Pluto/Fixed Decanate

Sun in Cancer 10 Degrees to 19 Degrees

Approximately July 4 to July 13

Middle-decanate Cancers are influenced by the planet Pluto and tend to be sexy and obsessive. Pluto is always concerned with transforming you into a better person and with transforming the world into a place with more light and less shadow. That said, you may have a helluva time with transitions, as going from one extreme to another can be jarring to say the least!

The fixed influence makes you excellent at sticking to projects until they come to fruition, as well as staying in a relationship through the ups and downs. You work hard at what is important to you. What would help you be happier on a daily basis is to let as much friendship and frivolity into your life as you can. You are apt to be a bit of a loner, even if you have tons of friends. It will take effort for you to put your defenses down and let the ones who matter in. But it will be worth it. And make sure you don't allow your workaholic tendencies to take over. Choose fun, dammit!

Upcoming Outer Planet Transits

From mid-January 2029 through January 2038, Pluto in Aquarius will be making a quincunx aspect to your Sun. This can feel like a challenging square but with milder effects. However, I have often found the relationship between the signs of Cancer and Aquarius to be oddly loyal, unexpected, and compelling. The key is to seek out what you need from the sign of Aquarius in the big picture sense. Think about this: You, Cancer, are a Guardian who thrives when protecting what you believe to be valuable. Your focus tends to be more personal than global. Aquarius is very interested in global matters, and although somewhat cold in comparison to your warmth, really does make the world a better place en masse as opposed to one-on-one. See if you can borrow these skills while Pluto in Aquarius is transiting your Sun.

Third-Decanate Cancer:

The Neptune/Mutable Decanate

Sun in Cancer 20 Degrees to 29 Degrees

Approximately July 14 to July 23

Late-decanate Cancerians like you are influenced by dreamy Neptune. This gives you a certain magical but elusive quality. Love is the drug you crave the most. When you are in a relationship, you tend to go all in. You like to merge. During times when you are flying solo, or even when you are involved, make sure to spend "me time" not just getting Thai massages, but connecting with the real you. You are very good at putting on a pleasing front, but there are parts of you that live in the shadows that just want to be seen. Welcome them.

Upcoming Outer Planet Transits

From June 2030 to May 2033, disruptive and progressive Uranus will be priming you to finish up one cycle in your life to prepare for grand new beginnings. This transit is apt to stimulate your intellect and make you want to explore the link between technology and spirituality. It's a bold new time for a bold new you.

YOUR MERCURY SUPER SIDEKICK

Cancer Sun with Mercury in Cancer: You have a dreamy way of talking that most people find soothing. Even if you are just describing the bagel and cream cheese you had for breakfast, it sounds as if you are passing on great wisdom.

Cancer Sun with Mercury in Gemini: You have a quick wit and love to teach and learn. Cancers are emotional water signs, but the Gemini influence makes you much lighter in spirit. Mercury rules Gemini, so you may be a gifted writer and communicator as well as a shameless flirt.

Cancer Sun with Mercury in Leo: Cancers can be a little shy, but Leos rarely are. The influence of Leo here is apt to raise your charisma level, which is already pretty high. Power is an aphrodisiac, and the Leo vibes make people sense that you are the boss in the boardroom *and* the bedroom.

Leo the Leader

July 23 to August 22

Element: Fire

Mode: Fixed

Planet: Sun

SUPERPOWER: THE POWER TO INSPIRE

In the previous century and even during the opening decades of the twenty-first, you Leos were praised for your rock star charisma, your moves like Jagger (a Leo!) and such. But during the Pluto in Aquarius era, this new version of Earth needs more from you than a boa and a twerk. Leos possess grand leadership skills, just the gifts we require if we are to survive and thrive during these apocalyptic times. You've no doubt read about the energy of fire signs, and that description still holds true. But with the world on fire, the ante has gone up.

O Captain! Our Captain! So many people are afraid to get out front and make a statement. Not you, Leo. You have the chutzpah and the self-confidence to step up and take charge as the chaos of the world accelerates at an alarming rate. So what makes a good leader in this era?

Vision. You need to know what the endgame is to lead the troops. Think of yourself like a movie director. You have actors, writers, editors, cinematographers, set designers, costume designers, extras, and more—all looking to you to inspire them to contribute their gifts to the big picture. So get ready to holler, "Action!"

Writer and activist James Baldwin was a Leo, and his big heart and charismatic oratory helped solidify his place as a timeless intersectional writer and activist. Madonna is a pop icon whose performative charisma remains iconic. But she will also always have a place in the hearts of the LGBTQ community as a huge celebrity who used the spotlight to shed light on the devastation of the gay community during the AIDS era. You lead by example and teach people through example how to love others on a massive scale.

SUPERPARTNER POWER

As a lover, you preside mightily as king or queen—or what have you—of the jungle, you wild thing. Passion, intensity, and luxuriousness are your key words. Go big or go home. Jealousy is a bugaboo for you, but so long as you make it clear to your boo what your expectations are, you should be golden. Of course there are plenty of polyamorous Leos in this era, but that just means you want more attention from more people. In hierarchical poly relationships you may often find yourself at the top, of course, and you are likely so good to your lover(s) no one would dare de-throne or cockblock you.

You have a big heart, Leo, a quality that makes you a wonderful partner. Your ability to show warmth and affection makes your beloved feel adored and appreciated. If you are ever too smothering, a partner using good communication will tell you that, but for those who dig being in a romance that feels bigger than life, you are the one.

Considering how "big picture" and megawatt you are, lovers may be surprised by your talent for nuance. The quickie is not your style. Long, erotic deep dives into your partner's body make you a memorable romancer. And you too appreciate having your whole body given great attention. Leo rules the back, and this is a particular area you love to have worshipped.

Besides just being a good lay, you are a natural in a relationship. It's the famous Leo warmth that pulls in your partner, and it's your loyalty and integrity that inspires them to stick around.

SUPERCOMMUNITY POWER

Your platonic relationships are full of soul and substance as well. As we slowly journey through the Pluto in Aquarius cycle, friendships become even more important in our lives. As a pal, you are loyal and consistent and possess a solidity of character that makes your buds feel safe. Friends don't necessarily need a lot of words from you (and certainly no pontificating), but they do appreciate how you stand by them. Nobody's shoulder is stronger than yours.

In your tribe (family/community), your leadership skills really come into play. You have the confidence to take charge of group projects, plan festivities and impromptu soirees, and just make sure the gang's all here. It's not just about your organization skills (which you have plenty of), it's your heartfelt desire to bring people together that spreads to the whole bunch. Family is what you make it, and whether bio or chosen or intergenerational mishmash, you really know how to carve the communal tofurkey and make everyone feel welcome at the table.

SUPERSHADOW

When I am doing the chart of a Leo or discussing Leo planets in a client's chart, there are certain issues that come up regularly. Even though Leos have great potential for leadership, there is one thing that can often get in the way: a craving for attention. To release the old conditioning and get ready to accomplish great things for a New Earth, you really need to let the applause-seeking adolescent in you go. Notice I didn't say child, as your childlike spirit is beautiful. You maintain your sense of awe and playfulness throughout life, which is wonderful. But adolescence is a tricky time. It often involves staring into the mirror and believing that the world revolves around you. This is a stage of life, and it's normal. But you don't want to be the lone mid-life Leo who gets left behind as a better planet is being built just because you are in need of endless flattery.

The best way to deal with your shadow is to treat it like a young friend who is struggling. Ask it what it needs. It probably needs a type of attention that it fears you—the mature version of your Leo self—will view as "too much." It probably doesn't want to seem needy, so instead it acts out. Sometimes all this part of you requires is to be listened to. And you are a great listener, Leo.

SUPERFOES

THE ALL-ABOUT-ME MONSTER AND THE DRAMA QUEEN

Leo, the Leader, I want you to be extra-aware of two superfoes who may exist in your life or whom you may draw to you at different times in your journey.

First, the *All-About-Me Monster*: She has the innate ability to turn every conversation around so it revolves around her. She insists on total eye contact so she knows she has a psychically captive audience.

Second, *the Drama Queen*: He can't bear to leave anything low-key. He's got to exaggerate matters to bring attention to himself and insists on creating a roller coaster of emotion, just to fill some emptiness within.

Sound awful? Yes, but guess what? They are only showing you an extreme Bizarro version of yourself. They show up because you unconsciously draw them to you to show you a part of yourself you need to deal with. Perhaps you are not the full drag-wearing, over-the-top version of these characters. But if you show up with humor and tenderness for the All-About-Me Monster and the Drama Queen, they won't feel the need to harass you in full regalia anymore.

❋ MYSTICAL SUPERPOWERS ❋

Tarot

In the standard Rider-Waite tarot deck, we can look to the eighth major arcana card, Strength, to get a sense of the timeless god/dess-like powers of your zodiac sign. This is the big Leo card of the deck. The image portrayed is of a woman holding open the mouth of a lion—not something your average Jo would do! But Leo the Leader inspires all with her belief in herself and in the powerful animal. They are, after all, two sides of the same coin. The beauty and the beast. Strength also illustrates your potential destiny in matters of work and wealth. In these areas, your joie de vivre acts as a magnetic force for success and prosperity.

Kabbalah

ט

In ancient mystical Kabbalah, the ninth letter of the Hebrew alphabet, tet, corresponds to the sign of Leo. Its symbol—a snake curled in on itself—is associated with pure goodness and fertility. Like Leo's number—nine—fertility in humans is associated with the nine-month gestation period. Much as the Strength card described above suggests that true power rests in containment, *tet* suggests that nature has its cycles, which should be honored. And that includes human nature!

In the Kabbalistic Tree of Life, Leo, strength, and tet are connected to the nineteenth path on the human journey. These paths connect the ten sefirot—or divine attributes—to each other. This is the path between Chesed, the fourth sefirah—or sphere—in the Tree, which represents mercy, and Gevurah, the fifth sefirah, which represents severity.

This is a path you were born to walk, Leo. You are known for your generosity and huge heart. No leader could inspire in any significant way without those qualities. And yet Gevurah is the other piece of the puzzle. It must be severe in its dedication to boundaries and rules. To "cheat" would not be fair.

In Kabbalistic astrology, Leo corresponds with the month Av on the Hebrew calendar. Av is the fifth month, just as Leo is the fifth sign of the zodiac. The fifth house is associated with creativity, children, and the adolescent period of life. The Hebrew letters associated with Av are tet, the letter of fertility discussed above, and kaf, which in Hebrew translates to "crown." There is a childlike innocence to the fact that, yes, Leos can act and be treated like royalty, but more importantly, the most evolved Leos treat everyone they meet as if they could be a king or queen. Leos, you really do rule!

Your Magic Spell

When you have forgotten you are more than just human—you are a superhero of the infinite—use this magic spell:

Close your eyes and lift your face up toward the Sun (or use your imagination to do so), and say aloud or silently to yourself:

"I am a Leader. I inspire myself and the world to bring the warmth of the Sun into our lives. Universe, what is the most uplifting path for me to take?"

THE THREE SUPERDECANATES OF LEO

First-Decanate Leo:

The Solar/Fixed Decanate

Sun in Leo 0 Degrees to 9 degrees

Approximately July 23/24 to August 1/2

Oh, the most Leo of Leos! You darlings tend to be the most serious of the bunch. You have an extra dose of your ruling planet, the Sun, and you do tend to operate like Sun Kings or Queens. You tend to be the most goal oriented of Leos. You first-decanate souls tend toward black-and-white thinking when whipping your followers into a frenzy. This tendency to polarize can be dangerous and limiting. If you have a good deal of air (Gemini, Libra, Aquarius) and/or mutable signs (Gemini/Virgo/Sagittarius/Pisces) in your chart, you are likely to tone it down. The good side to this tendency is that you can be loyal to a fault and tenacious as they come.

Upcoming Outer Planet Transits

Pluto will be transiting the early degrees of Aquarius through mid-February 2031. This makes an opposition to your Sun, which calls for diplomacy. Don't push. When you feel that urge to try to steer things in your direction through force, or what you call *persuasion*, take a deep breath or count to ten. Then go with the flow or let the person or people you are dealing with take the lead. Yep, it's similar to the old saw "I don't chase; I attract." But in this case it's "I don't push; I receive." Face it, you would much prefer to have people lining up at your door to do your bidding than getting your way by force.

Second-Decanate Leo:
The Jupiter/Mutable Decanate

Sun in Leo 10 Degrees to 19 degrees

Approximately August 2/3 to August 11/12

Middle-decanate Leos also tend to have a little of the old-time religion or soulful spirituality inside them. Even if it's just an intellectual philosophy that sparks your fire, you are apt to become fanatical in a cute way about it!

In terms of your superpowers, you tend to use them in off-the-cuff ways. You can definitely inspire individuals and the masses, but you may prefer to teach, and/or be a lifelong learner rather than take up a guru position. Unlike the average Leo (as if such a person exists!), you are a little commitment-shy and would prefer freedom over power.

Since you are influenced by your fellow fire sign, Jupiter-ruled Sagittarius, a mutable sign, you tend to be a lot more adaptable and a little less determined than the other decanates. If you have a lot of fixed energy in your chart in the form of planets in Taurus, Leo, Scorpio, and Aquarius, you are apt to be a little more forceful.

Upcoming Outer Planet Transits

Uranus in Gemini is likely to spark a lot of change and progress in the way you experience love between 2026 and mid-May 2033. Gemini opposes the sign Sagittarius, which is ruled by Jupiter, the planet associated with middle-decanate Leos like you. It is likely that during this time you are drawn to lovers and companions who are superbrainy and quick-thinking. Intellect becomes an aphrodisiac for you.

Third-Decanate Leo:

The Mars/Cardinal Decanate

Sun in Leo 20 Degrees to 29 degrees

Approximately August 12/13 to August 22/23

Third-decanate Leos are influenced by passionate Mars. Physical activity is often a must, and the more intense, the better. Martial arts are a fabulous option for Mars-influenced Leos like you. You are likely competitive by nature but love the timeless vibe of ancient sports. Even if you are playing badminton you maintain an Olympian spirit and ability to focus and put yourself in the zone. Look out, birdie! You are Leo the Leader with the power to inspire, but you are also imbued with the energy of Mars-ruled Aries the Warrior, who possesses the power to take action. You are brave and bold and full of enthusiasm. Sometimes you act too fast, but more often than not, your take-charge spirit comes through as heroic. Aries is also a cardinal sign, representing leadership and initiative. If you have a good sampling of cardinal in your chart (Aries, Cancer, Libra, Capricorn), you will probably be extradecisive and keen to make bold moves. You don't need anyone's advice or approval. You go your own way.

Upcoming Outer Planet Transits

Good news for you, boo! Neptune's transit through Aries, which lasts until March 2039, is infusing these years with magic for you. Is there a form of creative expression or a mystical path you have always longed to experience? You are unafraid, so why not go for it? Just be aware that Neptune's vibe can sometimes be depressive. The antidote is to practice kind self-talk and use the practical part of your Leo nature to ascertain whether you are deluding yourself. The way to be sure is this: If you are feeling ungrounded, even if you are excited, it might be time to hit pause and meditate on your desires and plans.

YOUR MERCURY SUPER SIDEKICK

Leo Sun with Mercury in Cancer: You have Leo bravado, but it is tempered by a bit of introversion. You have the power to make others feel safe when you speak (and write).

Leo Sun with Mercury in Leo: Your charisma is exponentially higher than most people you'll meet, which gives you an irresistible star quality. Just make sure to turn up your warmth so you don't intimidate those close to you.

Leo Sun with Mercury in Virgo: You feel especially responsible for minding the details, and you always believe the buck stops with you. You are known for your integrity.

Virgo the Gardener

August 23 to September 22

Element: Earth

Mode: Mutable

Planet: Mercury

SUPERPOWER: THE POWER TO CULTIVATE

Virgo, you are a gardener who possesses the power to cultivate. So what does that mean? Well, as a gardener you are pleased to be tasked with the responsibility for preparing for your harvest. You love watching seeds sprout into fruit, vegetables, flowers, trees, and the like. There is something about doing things with your hands in the earth that feels natural and right. Even if you do not (yet) *literally* work with plants, you have the ability to cultivate and, of course, we are looking at being a gardener more as a metaphor for your new super-powered identity. That said, pick up that hoe, ho!

To cultivate is a beautiful way to say you have the power to grow and to elevate what you nurture and put your attention on. In times of an attention (or attention deficit!) economy, you have the ability to focus your attention on growing what you wish to bring to life. This could be in terms of a relationship, your wealth, your service to the world, or anything you decide.

You are known for your earth sign simplicity. Instead of throwing a mishmash of food into a pot (unless it's leftovers!), you use fresh, pure ingredients and trust they will elevate a simple dish into an elegant, healthy one. And as a mutable sign, you are adept at adapting. If something is out of season or unavailable, you use what you have with forethought, patience, and care.

Think of famous Virgos like Beyoncé and Zendaya, who are mutable in nature and maintain the ability to weave between personas while staying grounded in the relatability of who they really are. Pope Leo XIV and Mother Teresa fall under the sign of Virgo as well.

SUPERPARTNER POWER

You are so thoughtful, dear Virgo. Your gift for preparation is just another example of how you pay attention. If your partner, crush, bestie, what have you kvells over a vintage LP, a book, a game, or a bracelet they don't feel up for treating themselves to, you take note. And when their birthday or other occasion comes along, you present it in your humble, perfectly wrapped (even in tinfoil) way. Perhaps you waited for a sale or skipped a few dinners out because saving a buck is a priority for you, but you are not cheap with your attention.

You show love by truly *showing* love. Although you may be a wordsmith, verbally going on and on about your boo's eyes or thighs or talent for flute or making a dining room look cute is just not your style. Actions speak louder.

Romantically, you Virgos can take charge, but let's face it, it's also fun for you to follow your lover's lead. You may pretend to hide your fetishes, but you actually wear them on your G-string. If you have a lover who's open-minded, that is a plus. Being an earth sign, you may be intensely physical, and going too long without sex might drive you a bit crazy! Similarly, taking care of your body makes you feel much sexier. Eating right and staying fit are good for your mood and tend to put you *in the mood.* You are also great at self-improvement and cultivating this quality in your partner. Talk about added value!

SUPERCOMMUNITY POWER

As the archetype of the Gardener, you like to spend time cultivating what's valuable to you. Therefore, if a neighborhood or a service is important to you, whether it's feeding the children or saving the porcupines, you will be there! That means you could be the one organizing meetings and staying late to do the grunt work. What's so lovely about you, Virgo, is that you don't think of things like sweeping floors and collecting addresses to be menial. You really see God in the small things.

When it comes to friendships, you do best with regularity. A biweekly IRL with a close friend, long text convos with childhood buds on Tuesdays and Sundays—all that routine is just mother's milk to you. You need to make sure to use the main part of your ruler Mercury—communication—and really speak to your peeps. Don't multitask or go on autopilot. Just like when you are out in nature, make sure you cultivate *presence* with the human animals in your life.

✵ SUPERSHADOW ✵

Your critical nature can sometimes take over, even when you feel like you are just being helpful. Humans can be easily embarrassed (unless they have every planet in Sagittarius!) and feel ashamed when their flaws are pointed out. Of course you can give constructive criticism when asked, and if you lead with your head that's fine, especially in business. BUT, even in so-called neutral business situations, humans are involved, and your idea of improving someone's performance may lead them to worry that you think they're incompetent.

In personal life this can really lead to explosive situations. If someone has an anger problem, you might ask them to count to ten before speaking from a place of rage. But by the same token, could you count to ten before you let loose with a litany of helpful suggestions that might be dictated by your need to control the minutiae?

Try to do some shadow work in which you engage with that perfectionist part of you. What is the shadow afraid will happen if certain things in life are left messy or unplanned? Once you figure that out, you can rest assured you are being truly helpful, not just acting out of anxiety.

✵ SUPERFOES ✵

THE CAN'T-SEE-THE-FOREST-FOR-THE-TREES MONSTER AND THE NAGMEISTER

Unconsciously, we all embody foes whose particular brand of obnoxiousness gets our goat the most! The Can't-See-the-Forest-for-the-Trees Monster is so focused on the picayune and the inconsequential details, she fails to see the big picture. Imagine it's the night before your friend's wedding, and you notice a big zit on her forehead. You could just come over with the perfect concealer on the big day. But instead, you send her links on what to eat and not eat to prevent pimples. When she bursts into tears and rage, you continue pontificating about skincare. Don't you see that she is hours away from perhaps the most meaningful day of her life? So why aren't you being supportive instead of stirring up her anxiety? When you are becoming this monster, try asking this simple question of the other person: "Would you like some help? What would be most helpful right now?"

The Nagmeister is never satisfied and always has something petty to focus on. They love to remind you to get your car washed, call your brother, and throw out the yogurt that expired at midnight. Okay, this is not terrible; it's like a tic you can't control. But it's not like having a heart condition! Mindfulness is called for to make you less of a picky pest. You can practice the art of saying nothing or pausing before you nitpick.

Tarot

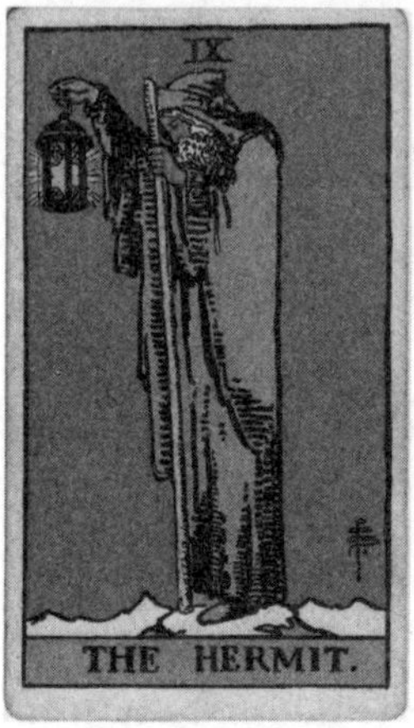

In the classic Rider-Waite tarot deck, Virgo is represented by the Hermit, the ninth trump card in the deck. It is portrayed as a figure in a long gray cloak holding a lantern. The Hermit can best be understood as a true sage, someone who has dedicated significant time to studying the invisible world and applying its wisdom to the natural world.

As a gardener archetype, you flourish when connecting with the world of nature, with buds and bulbs you can hold in your hands. The interesting thing to note is that your opposite sign, Pisces, is all about the invisible spiritual world. The Hermit seems to suggest that through your physical practices you get closer to the world of spirit.

Kabbalah

י

In the ancient mystical system of Kabbalah, Virgo is connected to the tenth Hebrew letter, yud. The primordial meaning of this letter teaches us about the spark of life that started the world. Virgo the Gardener, I think of it like a seed, and this seed grows fast. This is very fitting now in the second quarter of the twenty-first century, an era defined by its hyperspeed.

Yud sits on the Tree of Life path between Tiferet, the sefirot of beauty, and Chesed, the sefirot of mercy and compassion. Tiferet sits at the very center of the Tree of Life, and its position illuminates the need for the balancing of opposites. I see Chesed as the human, flawed voice that gently guides the abstract Tiferet in understanding that there is no perfection, just the movement *toward* perfection. Resonate much, Virgo? In other words, go within and accept imperfection as a kind of perfection, and when you emerge to connect with others, remember this and cut them some slack!

Virgo is associated with the Hebrew month of Elul, which interestingly enough is known for its position in the "seed-level state," a state of purity with the utmost potential. Kabbalistically, Virgo, it is wise to regularly return to your seed state and ask yourself, "How would I like my garden to grow?"

Your Magic Spell

When you have forgotten you are more than just human—you are a superhero of the infinite—use this magic spell:

Touch a plant, a flower, or a tree and send it love (or use your imagination to do so), and say aloud or silently to yourself:

"I am a Gardener. I cultivate good health and growth for myself and the world.

Universe, what is the most wholesome path for me to take?"

First-Decanate Virgo:

The Mercury/Mutable Decanate

Sun in Virgo 0 Degrees to 9 Degrees

Approximately August 22/23 to August 31

As an early-decanate Virgo, you possess an extra helping of Virgo traits. So how does your garden grow? Well, you choose your words carefully but intuitively, which is a very cool feat! You have the magical ability to speak things into existence. The old mystics teach us that the word *spelling* is no accident. When we speak, we cast a spell. Most people, however, just blather on. You actually are an alchemist of communication. You say just enough for your words to truly matter—no more, no less. Also, with a double dose of Virgo energy, the bawdy earth sign in you comes out more often than one might expect. You bring a whole new refresh to dirty talk!

Upcoming Outer Planet Transits

Uranus, the planet of optimism, disruption, and progress, is traveling through the early degrees of Gemini through early July 2028. There are two interesting things going on here. First, you have a strong connection to Gemini, as you are both ruled by Mercury, the sign of communication. While Mercury maintains a sole focus on language, you tend to express your message through action, particularly related to the natural and physical world. You are also more driven to serve. Gemini squares your Sun, and square angles call for compromise. Perhaps you can do a little less and say a little more?

Second-Decanate Virgo:

The Saturn/Cardinal Decanate

Sun in Virgo 10 Degrees to 19 Degrees

Approximately September 1 to September 10

Middle-decanate Virgos are under the influence of Saturn, ruler of Capricorn. You tend to be more diplomatic and less fussy than your Virgoan sibs, and you speak with more authority. You emanate ambition and have your eye on a long-term prize. You probably like your sex smoldering, and then it's back to work.

Your reputation may be of the utmost importance to you, and you likely care a great deal about maintaining your dignity and the respect of your peers. If it sounds like I'm saying that you take yourself very seriously, I am! But you know what? You have a serious agenda to accomplish much while attached to this mortal coil. And besides, you have a dry and deadpan wit that balances out your intensity.

Upcoming Outer Planet Transits

Uranus transits the middle degrees of Gemini from May 2028 through mid-August 2030. There are two interesting things going on here. First, you have a strong connection to Gemini, as you are both ruled by Mercury, the sign of communication. While Mercury maintains a sole focus on language, you tend to express your message through action, particularly related to the natural and physical world. Second, you are more driven to serve. Gemini squares your Sun, and square angles call for compromise. Perhaps you can do a little less and say a little more?

Third-Decanate Virgo:

The Venus/Fixed Decanate

Sun in Virgo 20 Degrees to 29 Degrees

Approximately September 11 to September 23

Late-decanate Virgos, you are often the most romantic and partner-oriented of the lot. With the influence of Venus, you likely find great happiness sharing your life with another. Simple things like cooking meals together and taking vacations where you make new memories are usually some of your favorite things. In some ways you are the simplest of the lot, and I mean that as a compliment.

Money is also a big motivator for you. You are influenced by fellow earth sign Taurus (ruled by Venus), and you can always enjoy the small pleasures more when your bank account has a comfortable balance. When you need to break out of your routine, Venus also makes music a big aphrodisiac for you. You probably know how to work on a dance floor too!

Upcoming Outer Planet Transits

Pluto is traveling through the late degrees of the fixed sign of Aquarius from mid-February 2035 through mid-January 2044. This transit is apt to influence you greatly. You are the fixed decanate of Virgo. Your challenge will be to develop trust in "flow" and not try to push events in your favor. The universe has your back, but when you try to force things, you're on your own. Practice the Daoist art of *wu wei* and believe that a bridge of incidents will gracefully take you to your destination. Give up a little control for true peace of mind and success.

✵ YOUR MERCURY SUPER SIDEKICK ✵

Virgo Sun with Mercury in Virgo: Mercury is Virgo's ruler, so you are blessed with a very favored placement of your communication planet. You can stay on message, and you win hearts and minds by your combination of logical, clear-sighted thinking and your willingness to roll up your sleeves and do whatever you can to pitch in.

Virgo Sun with Mercury in Leo: Having your communication planet in Leo likely gives you a more extroverted quality than the typical Virgo. Your language and IRL energy are bigger than life, and you don't mind being the center of attention.

Virgo Sun with Mercury in Libra: The influence of Libra makes you more aesthetically minded and may infuse your voice with dulcet tones. Your speech is seductive, and you tend to give compliments more than the typical Virgo.

Libra the Artist

September 23 to October 22

Element: Air

Mode: Cardinal

Planet: Venus

SUPERPOWER: THE POWER TO HARMONIZE

Libra, you are the Artist, the person who can take even the uglier aspects of life and shift them into balance to bring out what is beautiful and meaningful. To be an artist is to blend creative, personal expression with strong critical thinking. You may indeed be a literal artist, as many Libras are blessed with creativity and especially well-honed aesthetic and visual sense. But you do not have to practice art using paint or dance or another medium. Indeed, to be an artist in the grandest, most human sense means to make the living of life an art form in and of itself—to elevate the world through a day-to-day appreciation of beauty, the finer things, and love.

What does it mean to harmonize? This superpower is subtle and nuanced like you, Libra. In music, to harmonize means to combine different sounds to reveal a new melodic texture. In relationships, to harmonize means to create a sense of equality and balance in which both people feel heard, seen, and valued. To harmonize in business means to unify the various parts into an efficient system that works to meet the goals of all the players. In all of these, the key is found in the combining and aligning of different forces to make a third entity that is stronger than its parts.

Libra John Lennon focused on peace over war and wore his love for Yoko Ono for all the public to see, even when Beatles fans griped about it. Oscar Wilde put a premium on aesthetics, but he went deeper than mere charm and wit. His quote, "We are all in the gutter, but some of us are looking at the stars," captures the seriousness with which he took beauty. Serena Williams broke barriers when she opened up the sport of tennis to African American women. And it all began with her harmonizing with her tennis icon sister, Venus (a Gemini ruled by Mercury, FYI).

SUPERPARTNER POWER

You are most likely a lover, not a fighter, and yet you can maintain a contrarian streak that pops up during disagreements. You have a reputation for being too accommodating, so I say, you go, Libra! Your sign is ruled by Venus, the planet of love, and relationships are your area of expertise. For you, having a partner on your arm is a key part of your happiness. You prioritize love and are willing to compromise to make it work. Being the Artist, you instinctively know how to beautify your romance. Your secret seems to be to play to its strengths.

It's fine with you if your partner sees you through rose-colored glasses, but you are pretty good at seeing your boo for who they are. And you can be particularly good at making them feel better about themselves. If we are using aesthetics as a metaphor, let's talk about negative space. In a photograph, let's say, the artist may seemingly focus on the image that occupies the most space in the frame. The negative space is not where the energy is placed, yet it holds a lot of the "silence" of the work of art. The same way a pause in a musical composition may seemingly contain no sound, it still contains *something* ineffable and important. So just make sure you are not so focused on harmonizing your love life that you avoid the not-so-obvious. You want to make sure you are honest with yourself and your partner if a small problem starts to grow.

Granted, this is all very abstract. But Libra, you are a cerebral one. If you need me to describe your loverly ways in layman's terms (or getting laid terms), I would say you are a lot more erotic than your chill exterior would belie. You are ready and willing for your partner, but underneath your ardor there is likely still a passion for fine dining, exotic vacations, and beautiful interior design that might turn you on even more than sex.

SUPERCOMMUNITY POWER

You are a terrific friend and community member, Libra. When pals want a light, cheery companion they turn to you, even if you rarely arrive on time. At least you look good. Balancing partnership and friendship is sometimes a juggle for you. When friends want time alone with you, it might be hard for them to find. This is an issue of nuance, but pay attention to signs that you are not creating harmony between these two worlds.

As a community member, you are very dedicated. You believe in justice and have very strong political opinions. You're the real deal. At the same time, what you may enjoy most about your local activism is the social-schmocial aspect. Ahem.

Libra, you are able to use your power to harmonize by staying loyal to diverse groups you believe in. Your diplomacy lends itself to long-term friendships with people who share some, if not all, of your beliefs. Civilized discussion about hot-button topics is something you are adept at.

SUPERSHADOW

Whenever I do a chart for someone with heavy Libra influence, I am reminded of the shadow that hangs over you beauteous peeps. The emotion that dare not speak its name is anger. This extreme issue can play out in a few different ways. For many Libras, it is something you avoid. When you get mad at someone you tend to swallow it to keep the harmony. However, this can only lead to one thing: resentment. Sometimes you Libras repress your anger so much that one day you just get up and leave, and the other person is left reeling because they couldn't read your mind. Some Libras can be supervolatile in their personal lives, and some may focus their rage into their work. Did I say lawyers? Don't sue me! Other Libras attract partners with a short fuse who "hold" the anger in the relationship so they don't have to. This is clearly a maladaptive, out-of-balance situation when it happens.

But I do have an exercise for you dear Libras to try when it comes to anger. Pick someone in your life who does not play a key role to experiment on. So rather than a spouse, child, boss, or parent, how about a friend you see once in a while who isn't in your inner circle, or a cousin with whom you have a neutral, low-key connection?

Let's say this person has a habit of picking the place you go out to lunch. You always love where they choose, but try asserting yourself in a tiny way by saying you'd like to pick the spot this time. And then do it again. If you are a typical Libra, you are probably going to worry that they will be mad at you. Of course they won't! Explore being assertive as if it is akin to slowly releasing air out of a bicycle tire. You will become more comfortable and less afraid. And then when you do have to get into it with someone whose life is closely intertwined with yours (spouse, boss, etc.), you will be able to speak your mind more easily and without so much worry about the consequences. One thing to keep in mind—your blind spot, really—is that your idea of aggression is, to most people, more like a tap on the arm. In most cases, you think standing up to someone over something small is like punching them in the face, when most of the time it is no big deal. Anger dysmorphia!

SUPERFOES

THE PASSIVE-AGGRESSIVE MONSTER AND THE SUPERFICIALIZER

So you like to be liked and love to be loved, which makes you someone who at times is very risk-averse. If you have someone in the bag, be it a romantic partner, friend, colleague, etc., you may not want to rock the boat (see the anger issue insights above). So what do you do? Instead of fighting (i.e., being aggressive), you have an inner monster who slowly gaslights others by not fighting. And yet, those little snipes and fibs to keep the peace can become downright mean if they go unchecked. A good way to deal with this Passive-Aggressive Monster is to allow yourself to feel your feelings. Maybe you are sad about not feeling understood but scared to express those feelings. At least allow yourself to cry, to feel the sadness. You will make space within yourself to then say what is really going on instead of making the other person guess.

And then there is your other foe, the one you embody as the Superficializer. To avoid any potential conflicts, you stick to what you know: the weather, the latest gossip, and an occasionally tedious inventory of other obvious subjects. What a shame! People really do want to see you and be seen, but this monster shuts down true connection with a lot of inane blather! When you hear yourself speaking only in fluff, remind yourself that you are more than just your ability to please and that nothing is more pleasing than the real you!

✵ MYSTICAL SUPERPOWERS ✵

Tarot

In the classic Rider-Waite tarot deck, Libra rules the eleventh major arcana card, Justice. A figure sits on a throne holding scales in one hand and a sword in the other. The card is primarily red, emanating passion and life force. But the objects she holds suggest a need for discernment. Libras are tasked with being artists of the social contract. You can set an example for others by finding that balance of considering yourself and your needs, while also considering those of the whole. Your relationship with justice, Libra, is subtle and lifelong.

You are an expert at using sound judgment in the myriad situations that arise in life. You don't need any advice from the Justice card. Think of it as a reminder to stick to your sense of values and integrity, allow all parties to speak their mind, and then look for the common feelings between all.

Kabbalah

ל

In the ancient wisdom system of Kabbalah, Libra is associated with the twelfth letter in the Hebrew alphabet: lamed. *Lamed* translates to "prod," as in to prod someone to move forward, to teach to learn. Lamed has an airy association, so that the forward motion is more of a mental rather than literal variety.

The path of Libra on the Tree of Life falls between Gevurah, the sphere of judgment and discernment, and Tipharet, the sphere of beauty and harmony. This path is so spot-on for the trajectory of life for you, Libra. You want pleasure, ease, and lack of conflict. But to ensure those things, you must exhibit strength and a strong sense of boundaries.

The month of Tishrei is Libra's month, Kabbalistically speaking. Tishrei is ruled by Venus, just like Taurus, with whom you share your ruling planet. This month has many spiritual celebrations, and it is a reminder to you, Libra, to balance your love of logic and rationality (air sign!) with an openness to your inner light and the invisible messages of the universe.

Your Magic Spell

When you have forgotten you are more than just human—you are a superhero of the infinite—use this magic spell:

Use your fingers to draw something balanced and beautiful in the air (or use your imagination to do so), and say aloud or silently to yourself:

"I am an Artist. I harmonize the varied influences upon myself and the world.

Universe, what is the most peaceable path for me to take?"

THE THREE SUPERDECANATES OF LIBRA

First-Decanate Libra:

The Venus/Cardinal Decanate

Sun in Libra 0 Degrees to 9 Degrees

Approximately September 22/23 to October 2

You value a pleasing social life and an aesthetically pleasing environment. The arts make you feel at peace. You may also need a lot of downtime and rest to make it through a mentally stimulating workday and a socially active nightlife. Your biggest craving, however, is for relationships. Standing on your own two feet scares you despite your cool front. Of course you have the power to fly solo, but addressing that fear of being alone is a wise idea. Regularly practice the art of self-love. (I mean using your heart, not your right hand, babe!)

Upcoming Outer Planet Transits

Uranus, Neptune, and Pluto will all be making pleasing aspects to your Sun through April 2029. You are an artist of balance, so make sure you don't emphasize one area of your life over another for too long. With fellow air signs Gemini and Aquarius in play, along with fire sign Aries, you are in a place where you can spread out your good fortune. Don't retreat from your desires out of fear.

Second-Decanate Libra:

The Uranus/Fixed Decanate

Sun in Libra 10 Degrees to 19 Degrees

Approximately October 3 to October 12

Libras born during the middle-decanate period are influenced by the sign Aquarius. Aquarius's ruler, Uranus, is pretty radical, so you are likely to be more extreme and fully committed than the typical balanced Libra. What you believe in means everything to you. Your values are pure, but sometimes you put people through unnecessary purity tests too. You tend to be ahead of your time and will find whole new areas of obsession as you explore technology, especially during this highly Aquarian era.

Upcoming Outer Planet Transits

March 2028 through March 2037 will find Pluto in Aquarius making a very harmonious trine aspect to your sign. Pluto encourages you to face your demons, let them go, and then do what you are meant to do on earth. Take a lesson from the sign Aquarius and be a visionary in your public pursuits. Relationships may take unconventional turns during this cycle, and you should be open to expanding the ways in which you love.

Third-Decanate Libra:

The Mercury/Mutable Decanate

Sun in Libra 20 Degrees to 29 Degrees

Approximately October 13 to October 22/23

Third-decanate Libras are highly influenced by Mercury, the planet of communication. Expressing yourself through language is highly favored. You also tend to have your ear to the train tracks in terms of trends and social change. You are tapped into the zeitgeist. The mutable influence of Mercury makes you especially flexible. You are a citizen of the world, able to adapt to a variety of cultures and belief systems.

Upcoming Outer Planet Transits

From June 2030 to July 2032, the influence of Uranus, the planet of progress known as "the great disruptor," will be stirring up a strong desire for freedom and change. You may feel a much greater urge to serve the world with your powers of diplomacy and intellect. Follow those desires! You may find yourself on a highly successful path, one in which you could change the course of history.

✵ YOUR MERCURY SUPER SIDEKICK ✵

Libra Sun with Mercury in Libra: You speak softly and don't carry a stick. Your double dose of Libra gives you an especially melodious voice and a desire to keep the vibe light and airy. You are well versed in arts and culture, and you excel at cocktail party conversations.

Libra Sun with Mercury in Virgo: You are more sarcastic than the average Libra, and you pay more attention to detail. Your communication skills tend to be sharp thanks to Mercury's connection with Virgo. Virgo being an earth sign mixed with flirty Libra suggests that body language is a big part of your vibe.

Libra Sun with Mercury in Scorpio: Mercury in Scorpio is sharp-tongued and critical but also deep and passionate. Adding this placement to your Sun in Libra suggests you are inspiring when you speak and less afraid to rock the boat than the typical Libra.

Scorpio the Shaman

October 23 to November 21

Element: Water

Mode: Fixed

Planet: Pluto

SUPERPOWER: THE POWER TO TRANSFORM

Shamans are like doctors. But instead of merely tending the body, they heal the spirt. The word originates from the Evanki language, a Tungusic tongue spoken in Siberia. It refers to a master of healing who innately perceives the meaning of the universe and uses this knowledge to heal the soul. Every community needs a shaman. Hell, there should be a shaman on every block, just like a coffee joint!

The superpower of Scorpio the Shaman is the power to transform, to change the very essence of something, not just its superficial appearance. Since you are a person of depth, Scorpio, of course just a surface glow-up would not suffice! Some say people don't change. But many a Scorpio does indeed change, not just by quitting smoking or becoming less guarded, but by transmuting a primal fear into a fundamental strength. You are capable of doing this for yourself, for others . . . for the whole world.

You simply *know* things, Scorpio. Your frequency is tuned in to the invisible world, which allows you to make yourself a more evolved person and the world a better place—if you choose to. You seek the truth at all costs.

Scorpios who possess this quality include artists Robert Mapplethorpe and Pablo Picasso. Talk about lightning rods! Speaking of lightning rods, former Secretary of State and first lady Hillary Clinton is a Scorpio, and so is musician Björk. Intense doesn't even begin to describe the nature of a typical Scorpio!

I remember seeing an interview with Björk after she was nominated for an Oscar for her leading role in Lars von Trier's *Dancer in the Dark*. She was brilliant in the role, though she was mocked later for wearing her whimsical swan dress to the ceremony! If you see the film you will feel how utterly committed she was to her character's heartbreaking tale. She was asked if she would do more acting, and she said no. She felt an awareness that time is limited, and she can only make so many albums in a lifetime; therefore, she'd rather focus her energy on music. Scorpios like Björk possess great courage, strength to stand up to the herd, and a willpower that ensures they can accomplish whatever they set out to do.

Another Gen X female singer, Natalie Merchant, is an example of the way in which a Scorpio can use their power for the greater good. You won't find her albums filled with breakup songs. Instead, she focuses on the world around her. She brings a poppy sweetness to her voice and music that lures us gently into thinking about how we can be more empathic and altruistic. Remember, Scorpio, as the Shaman you are not afraid to delve into the deepest emotional and spiritual waters. By doing so you lead by example, showing others that transforming into one's best self is truly possible.

SUPERPARTNER POWER

Intimacy means a lot to you. You see and sense all, and you want to be seen in return. But you are a complicated character, Scorpio. A mystery wrapped in an enigma even to yourself!

Scorpio, you have a sexy reputation, and it's well earned. You bask in the art of seduction and are able to keep this up throughout a relationship with the intrigue and mystery you purposefully dream up! You are charismatic and draw people to you easily, but you don't always trust so easily. Drawn more to commitment than flitting around, you may like your relationships to be, shall we say, *extra*? You can also likely go for long periods without a partner if you sense that the puzzle pieces just don't fit together.

You tend to have two speeds in love: all in or tortured poet. Sometimes in the same day! What you truly long for is to know another person's ins and outs, from the old in-out, in-out to what lies beneath the multitude of layers. Revealing yourself can sometimes be a sticky affair. You say you want to, but your focus on soaking up the essence of another makes it seem like maybe you don't. Despite being strong and decisive by nature, you may find that you confuse yourself in the ways you handle matters of the heart.

If you have a tantric lover who will explore the line between sex and spirituality, you will do well. If that person also shares the same day-to-day interests as you, all the better. As a water sign, you are often fraught with emotion, but having an earthy home base balances you out. At the end of the day, it is your raucous humor and tender teddy bear ways beneath the bluster that give you staying power.

SUPERCOMMUNITY POWER

You believe in chosen family, and that includes friends and community members. Since you tend to think in extremes about the best or worst possible things happening, you are likely to look at your besties as the people you may share a foxhole with one day and a penthouse the next. If the community needs you, you are there.

Friends know that you excel in times of crisis. If a pal is having a breakdown, you are there to offer up your Shamanistic skills to help them see this as a breakthrough. Never preachy, you come through with real healing. And if your pal just needs a listener, you can sit and just let them release.

On the lighter side, you are hilarious!

So for day-to-day fun, Scorpio, you are on call to laugh long and hard at whatever the current ridiculous events are. Although you have an introverted side that just wants to disappear into your lair, you also excel as an extrovert when you are in the mood to party. Then it is you surrounded by friends, dressed in costume, and ready to boogie!

SUPERSHADOW

Your depth and goodness along with your magnetism and charisma are your calling cards, Scorpio, but you know yourself well and know how dark you can go. With all your intensity, you can work yourself into states of emotional turbulence that can scare yourself and others. Your nervous system is tightly wound, and although you can meditate and peace out until the cows come home, there is also that side of you that just explodes when someone or something gets in your face.

Rather than push that side of you down and pretend it doesn't exist, or live in shame and regret over misjudged moments, there are other options.

First, remind yourself that living well is the best revenge. Being the best you and creating the best life feels so much better than pushing back against what angers you.

Since you are so adept at being there for your friends, find one who can listen to you and your worst fears. In addition, being that friend to yourself and writing about your feelings can help more than I can say.

Figure out what triggers you. Often it's a loss of control or a feeling of being disrespected. The latter ignites the street fighter in you. But you can adjust your perspective to see yourself as a member of an elite club, not a gutter gang!

The secret weapon you can always use to make peace (like the paradox?) is one you are going to love. It's called the high road. No, not in the *pass the dutchie* sense. Rather, taking the high road gives you a sense of contentment. Knowing you are being appreciated for letting things go is a big deal to you. It helps you sleep well at night. And if you need something petty in your pocket, here's a laugh: Your foes will be so mad when you make them look bad by being such a high roader!

✵ SUPERFOES ✵

THE MOODY MONSTER AND THE POSSESS-INATOR

Your nervous system is wired in an unpredictable way, and sometimes your moods get the better of you. That's when the Moody Monster comes out. People can feel his arrival a mile away and tense up in fear. The Moody Monster needs time alone to recharge (sleep! meditate!), even if it's just for 10 minutes. A little time-out goes a long way.

The Possess-inator is your brooding big brother. He is a hero, but sometimes he does not like to share the people in his life. And he may close in a little too strongly on those he loves. You can help the Possess-inator by showing him that everything he needs exists within. A good approach is developing a gratitude practice. Even if the Possess-inator only repeats "I have wonderful friends who all love me" three times, he will feel secure enough to unlock the handcuffs.

✵ MYSTICAL SUPERPOWERS ✵

Tarot

The tarot card Scorpio corresponds with is called Death. Despite the way it's been used in some cheesy horror films, it is not about literal death. It's about a major change. There are two cards in the tarot that represent change. The Tower symbolizes a sudden, shocking change. Death is more about a change that is big but that we expect. Think of the way a student graduates at the end of their final semester.

It's a big deal, but it's not a shock. When the Death card arises, I tend to pull a second card to illuminate what kind of change is in store. In the classic Rider-Waite tarot deck, a rider dressed in black armor sits astride a white horse. The extremes of black and white represent life's polarities. Scorpio is well positioned to navigate these polarities.

Kabbalah

נ

In the ancient mystical system of Kabbalah, Scorpio is associated with the fourteenth primordial Hebrew letter, nun. Nun corresponds to the number fifty, which represents the gates of knowing. Nun shows you that you stand on the precipice of believing you have a deeper perception of the invisible world, of actually *knowing* this deep in your bones.

In Kabbalah, Scorpio is connected to the month of Marcheshvan, associated with the Roman god of war. That said, your feelings about war can best be summed up by Scorpio President Teddy Roosevelt, who said, "Speak softly and carry a big stick." Since Scorpios of all genders possess big dick energy, I'm sure that resonates! Your power speaks for itself.

On the Tree of Life, Scorpio travels the path between Tipharet, the sefirot of beauty and harmony, and Netzach, the sphere of endurance. You know you have the ability to take the long road and overcome any obstacles to reach your goal. You just need to remember to stop and smell the roses along the path.

Your Magic Spell

When you have forgotten you are more than just human—you are a superhero of the infinite—use this magic spell:

Place a few drops of water on your solar plexus (or use your imagination to do so), and say aloud or silently to yourself:

"I am a Shaman. I transform the dark into the light for myself and the world.

Universe, what is the most miraculous path for me to take?"

THE THREE SUPERDECANATES OF SCORPIO

First-Decanate Scorpio:

The Pluto/Fixed Decanate

Sun in Scorpio 0 Degrees to 9 Degrees

Approximately October 23 to November 1

You are the most Scorpionic of Scorpios! Ruled by Pluto, you've likely known since childhood that you were different. It's the Shaman in you which is cranked up to eleven. When you are serving others as a healer or expressing yourself with complete authenticity, you are a dream to be around, and you feel most at home in your own skin. Never let the masses dictate who you should be. You may be a strong flavor, but when you own that truth you are delicious to yourself, your friends, and the world. Your challenge is to let down your defenses. The real you is a real gem.

Upcoming Outer Planet Transits

Pluto, your planetary ruler, will be transiting the early degrees of Aquarius through February 2031. You are apt to feel more powerful and tapped in than ever, and you are. However, you are really being called upon to use your Shamanistic powers to help the world and to evolve into the best version of yourself you can.

Second-Decanate Scorpio:

The Neptune/Mutable Decanate

Sun in Scorpio 10 Degrees to 19 Degrees

Approximately November 2 to November 11

Middle-decanate Scorpios, you are highly sensitive and intuitive and tend to need a lot of solitude. Artistic expression is necessary for your sanity! It can come in any form you like, but the idea is: You can't just operate on a literal level. The languages of symbols and mathematics speak to you, and you need to share who you are using magical means.

Your empathy is boundless, and you do best when you are allowing others to lean on you. Giving makes you stronger and more confident, and helps you soften your own shadows.

Upcoming Outer Planet Transits

You will feel the influence of Pluto (Scorpio's ruler) most between March 2028 and March 2038. Pluto will be transiting fellow fixed sign Aquarius during that cycle. This gives you an intense motivation to use your Shamanic superpower to transform the world. Neptune, the planet that rules your decanate, will influence you most strongly between March 2029 and March 2036. Use your intuition and your creative talents to the max.

Third-Decanate Scorpio:

The Mars/Cardinal Decanate

Sun in Scorpio 20 Degrees to 29 Degrees

Approximately November 12 to November 21/22

The influence of Mars makes you want to fight! Luckily, that aggressive energy can be put to great use in more constructive ways. Whether it's athletics or game theory, adventuring or obsessing over something that fascinates you, you have many means to stop yourself from resorting to verbal or physical fisticuffs! Not only were you born during the Mars decanate of Scorpio, but Scorpio itself is co-ruled by Mars, though that's not focused on so much in the twenty-first century. All that to say, you likely have quick reaction times and should seek out as many physical outlets for your energy as you can.

Upcoming Outer Planet Transits

Being a Mars-influenced Scorpio, it is important to note that two key outer planets will be transiting Mars-ruled Aries in the years to come. Saturn, the planet of structure and discipline, will be in Aries through April 2028, and Neptune, the planet of healing and imagination, will be in Aries until March 2039. You will feel Neptune's influence the most from mid-February 2034 to the end of its cycle five years later. During this time, pay more attention to the invisible world, as the universe will be sending you downloads up the wazoo!

✴ YOUR MERCURY SUPER SIDEKICK ✴

Scorpio Sun with Mercury in Scorpio: Sharp-tongued are you Mercury in Scorpio folk, but quick-witted and sexy too. Your body language and your lusty vibes make you irresistible. Your mind is always operating on a multitude of levels, and so are your words. Use your charisma with a smile and cut down on the rough tone.

Scorpio Sun with Mercury in Libra: Smooth operator. Seductive. Hypnotic. These words describe the way you use words! You have a tendency to speak softly, and many people may assume you are flirting with them. But no one can ever catch you at this game! If they try, you just pull a Libra and smile innocently and say, "What are you talking about?"

Scorpio Sun with Mercury in Sagittarius: Funny! The lightness of your neighbor Sag makes you the Scorpio most likely to guffaw and to make inappropriate jokes. You are fun and love to speak in different tongues. There is something ineffably exotic about you.

Sagittarius the Traveler

November 22 to December 22

Element: Fire

Mode: Mutable

Planet: Jupiter

SUPERPOWER: THE POWER TO EXPLORE

Sagittarius, you are known as a good-time Charlie. You're restless and on the make for experiences of all kinds. Freedom is your middle name. Your superhero archetype of the Traveler does not just apply to literal jet-setting, although your passport is indeed full of stamps. Beyond just the fun of going on excursions, you are a Traveler who seeks to explore the world, not just physically but mentally and spiritually too.

The power to explore encompasses a passion for discovery of new ways of life, belief systems, and more. There is an innate optimism you possess, Sag, which allows you to follow uncharted paths on your travels. You trust the universe to have your back and believe that strangers can soon become friends. This attitude in itself is a self-fulfilling prophecy!

Your ruling planet, Jupiter, is thought of as the planet of good luck and expansion. As a citizen of the world, you attract good luck through your open-minded and openhearted energy. Even if you are homebound for months or years, you still use your brain, heart, and spirit to explore the unknown. As a Traveler, you innately understand that what's in front of us, what's familiar, is merely a snapshot taken with a close-up lens. Everything else needs a wide-angle, in fact, a panoramic view.

You also are able to make mistakes in public and not fall apart. Musicians from Ozzy Osbourne to Taylor Swift have all dealt with the mocking of the media, only to maintain their good humor and come back to the spotlight with more respect than before. Sag author Jane Austen showed how the silly foibles of human nature can often lead to a good laugh but also a good-hearted relationship. And internationally acclaimed martial artist Bruce Lee embodied another strong element of the Sagittarian character: He delved deeply into philosophy. As a Traveler, Sagittarius, you possess the power to explore the physical as well as the invisible universe. As long as you are learning (and teaching!), you are happy.

SUPERPARTNER POWER

You kids are the most playful, silly lovers who bring a lot of joy to romance. Spontaneity is likely your thing, which makes you an energizing person to be around. People fall in and out of love with you quickly, and you do the same. You are as innocent, rambunctious, and lovable a companion as a puppy.

That said, you are a good dog, but you need a long leash! After all, you are a born explorer. Having fun and frolicking can make you a great romantic partner. But you may also find that being in a relationship is not so natural for you, even after decades. Sag folk are often wild and friendly beasts who do not like to be domesticated. You can be in love and even live with and marry your boo, but you still need a lot of space. Space to do what? Disappear into your own interests, go out with your buds, take trips solo, and maybe even flirt as much as you want to with other babes. If your partner could see inside your head, they'd know it's nothing personal. But it can be a hard instinct to explain without open and honest communication from both parties.

You do best with a partner who is also a freedom-loving kind. But of course, human nature being what it is, sometimes you may be attracted to a monogamist homebody with jealousy issues! Why? Because you are lovable as all hell, but also love to drive people crazy.

You may do well in an open relationship or one in which friendship comes first. And as a friend, you are great, but you may not like to go too deep. If a bud is on the skids, you're more likely to take them out for a drink and laugh rather than offer a shoulder to cry on. Being upbeat and positive is just how you roll.

Luckily, that means that even your exes speak well of you and are fine being friends. And it also means you may hit on said exes while sharing laughs over libations!

SUPERCOMMUNITY POWER

You are a justice-seeker by nature. Politics and religion are likely important subjects to you, and you may take them to the extreme. This means even if you are an anarchist or apolitical, an atheist or an agnostic, you still manage to harp on these subjects with fanaticism. You just love being a fanatic! This makes you a strong presence in the community, as you like to take action, not just talk the talk. You will actively go out and lead the legions if it's for something you believe in.

Using your powers of exploration, you can often suggest solutions to problems in your community, or in the world, that you have discovered through your travels. Your experiences may seem rambling and random to some, but you've actually seen or studied (or both) much of the world. You love to teach and learn, and these skills are excellent when the neighborhood gang needs some inspo and direction.

SUPERSHADOW

There's no doubt you are generous of spirit and prefer to forgive and forget rather than hold a grudge. However, beneath your affable, slick charm and surface warmth, you can be a real cold dude! We all have shortcomings, so the question is, why is this your big one? Well, you aren't known for your anger except for occasional blowups that pass quickly, but underneath your good nature, rage can grow quietly.

So when someone really needs you and you act removed, or if they call you on your seeming lack of empathy, you get grade-A pissed off. The way it might go in your head: *I am always doing favors and kindnesses for this a-hole, and now she's saying I don't care? WTF?* But being there, heart and soul, during a moment of need—or a long, tedious cycle of need—is very different from picking up the check or taking your bestie's dog for walks while they're away. You are considerate and thoughtful about helping people out in mundane ways, but sometimes things that call for a show of emotion and commitment are harder for you.

What folks may not realize is that you *will* come around most of the time, but you are not good dealing with serious emotions on the spot. You need space to intellectualize a good response!

More than anything, however, you can be the absolute worst at being called on your sh*t. If you've been a bad boy or girl—you know, if you've done something wild and reckless—*that* you can cop to. In fact, you are proud of those transgressions, as they seem cool. But if you are accused of being heartless, you may have a tendency to double down on coldness. If you were secure in your ability to really show up emotionally for those you love, you wouldn't take the hyperbole to heart. You'd know that the other person is just a temporary wreck and will be apologizing to you soon for getting worked up during a moment of crisis. But deep down, you are terrified that you really *don't* know how to act in adult emotional relationships. And hey, maybe you do have some work to do. But you know what? You are always growing, and with your largesse of spirit, you can certainly make a commitment to learning these skills. And yes, I did use the word *commitment* just to bug ya!

SUPERFOES

THE AVOID-INATOR AND CAPTAIN INSENSITIVE

You love a good debate and can have fun trading snappy comebacks and intriguing info with someone who takes the other side. However, when it comes to more personal matters, you prefer to leave your loved one on "read" while you go about your sunny and fun business for the day. That's the Avoid-inator in you! When difficult feelings arise, moving toward your loved one rather than away is superhard once the Avoid-inator takes over. Fight this foe with all the love in your heart!

As for Captain Insensitive, well, it's like this: The old Captain just can't read a room when there's only two people in it. At your best you keep everyone laughing, but that's usually out in public. At home or even in bed you sometimes forget the other person's emotional nature and proclivity for embarrassment. This does not make Captain Insensitive evil, but it does make her oblivious! The best way to neutralize this negative habit? Own up to it before anything happens with a line like, "Sometimes I go too far goofing around, so let me know if that happens. I think you're great!"

✵ MYSTICAL SUPERPOWERS ✵

Tarot

Sagittarius rules the fourteenth major arcana card, Temperance. It is a card that signifies healing of the spirit by taking the high road. In the classic Rider-Waite tarot deck, Temperance is portrayed as an angel in white, wings and all. She wears a breastplate that contains the four Hebrew letters of God: yud, hei, vav, hei. When Temperance comes up, I see it as a message to take the Sagittarian gift for exploration and turn that superpower toward oneself. *Tikkun olam* in Kabbalah means "heal oneself" and "heal the world." Although Sagittarius is the Traveler, one must be healthy and steady to travel without mishaps. This card has a lot of mystical esoteric associations, which could inspire you to think of yourself as an alchemist healing yourself.

Kabbalah

ס

In the ancient mystical system of Kabbalah, Sagittarius is associated with the fifteenth primordial Hebrew letter, samech. *Samech* translates to "support" and is closely aligned with concepts of interdependence and providing sustenance. The letter has a somewhat circular shape and conjures up the energy of a never-ending story.

On the Kabbalistic Tree of Life, Sagittarius can be found on the path between Tipharet, sefirot of beauty and harmony, and Yesod, the sefirot of foundation. Yesod is located on the lower half of the Tree, closer to the earth. I see this as the need to establish a firm foundation made of values and a structured life. Without those things, we are just reaching toward beauty and harmony, never really connecting with those concepts in a meaningful way. For you, Sag, think about making a home within your heart, and in the actual world, as you reach for the heights of transcendence. Otherwise, you just set yourself up for a fall.

In Kabbalah, Sagittarius is connected to the Hebrew month of Kislev. Kislev is thought of as the month of faith and miracles. At your best, Sag, you are a Traveler to many places who practices a form of faith that is specific to your heart and beliefs, and that allows you to truly cocreate with the universe and create miracles here on earth.

Your Magic Spell

When you have forgotten you are more than just human—you are a superhero of the infinite—use this magic spell:

Run in place until you feel your body warming up (or use your imagination to do so), and say aloud or silently to yourself:

"I am a Traveler. I explore the planet to learn the meaning of life for myself and the world.
Universe, what is the most adventurous path for me to take?"

THE THREE SUPERDECANATES OF SAGITTARIUS

First-Decanate Sagittarius:
The Jupiter/Mutable Decanate

Sun in Sagittarius 0 Degrees to 9 Degrees

Approximately November 22 to December 1

Early-decanate Sag peeps, you are the purest kind of Sag there is! You shoot from the hip, laugh the loudest, and with Jupiter influencing you big time, you also are the luckiest. This is not a surprise, as generous people tend to be very lucky. You are likely gregarious and extroverted, although you secretly study highly cerebral texts any chance you get. Of all the Sagittarians, you tend to be the most philosophical. No matter how wild you were in your salad days, as you age, you grow more fascinated by the question "What does it all mean?" You explore these questions of the nature of existence with great passion. But you can still stick a swizzle stick between the gap in your teeth.

Upcoming Outer Planet Transits

Uranus will be transiting the first decanate of Gemini through early May 2029. Gemini opposes your Sun and brings out great opportunities for you, so long as you can move out of your comfort zone. Start by expanding your definition of what a great relationship is. You can try anything that feels fresh and positive and full of goodwill. Just don't stay on autopilot! In your worldly pursuits, it's time to cull your message to the length of a logline. Help people understand your vision, and they will get behind you to a huge degree.

Second-Decanate Sagittarius:
The Mars/Cardinal Decanate

Sun in Sagittarius 10 Degrees to 19 Degrees

Approximately December 2 to December 11

Middle Sag folks like you tend to have excess physical energy. It's the influence of Mars, which can also make you an animal in bed. Just make sure you add some nuance to your moves! Cardinal energy affects you by making you a very strong leader. You work for causes you believe in and are happy to take charge of tricky situations, as you are nothing if not courageous. Patience may not be your strong suit, but by the same token you don't mind if someone tells you to shut up and listen! You can be blunt, and you respect directness in others as well.

Upcoming Outer Planet Transits

Since Mars—the ruler of Aries—has a big influence over you, it is a good idea to work with the energy of Neptune in Aries between April 2033 to July 2033. Neptune is thought of as the planet of healing and imagination. Rather than irrationally sticking to your uber-rational approach to life and art, make the most of your intuition! Explore what you sense has happened and will happen in society. Don't be afraid to be ahead of the curve. The rest of the world will catch up.

Third-Decanate Sagittarius:

The Sun/Fixed Decanate

Sun in Sagittarius 20 Degrees to 29 Degrees

Approximately December 12 to December 21/22

Late-decanate Sagittarians are the most ambitious and steadfast. The Sun's influence makes you want to shine in a very public way. You have a lot to share with the world and the confidence to do so. Having a fixed influence means you are better than the average Sag at working on a project, a relationship, a goal with a good deal of staying power. You understand how to finish things. Your faith shows itself by the way you approach a dream with single-minded focus. Your adorable weakness is likely a need for adulation!

Pluto, the planet of self-transformation, will be making a very inspiring sextile aspect to your Sun from April 2034 through early March 2044. You must release any shame you are carrying around so you can make room for more self-love. Once you feel truly proud of who you are, warts and all, mistakes and all, you will be able to share your vision with the world. You will feel seen while making others feel seen and understood as well.

YOUR MERCURY SUPER SIDEKICK

Sagittarius Sun with Mercury in Sagittarius: You possess a double dose of wild Sag energy. You are the ultimate raconteur and love to hold court for a crowd. Your endearing humor tends to make everyone feel like a friend. You may foot-in-mouth sometimes, but you also say the sweetest things!

Sagittarius Sun with Mercury in Scorpio: Mercury in Scorpio gives you more of an edge and brings out your serious side. This can come off as pretty blustery, but underneath your sharp rhetoric is deep passion. You express yourself with more emotion, and you tend to be more comfortable with intimacy than the average Sag.

Sagittarius Sun with Mercury in Capricorn: This Mercury placement makes you a little more cautious than most Sagittarians. You may not speak out of turn, especially where money and business are concerned. You communicate with wisdom, poise, and a worldly air. After two drinks, however, the dirty limericks begin!

Capricorn the Planner

December 23 to January 19

Element: Earth

Mode: Cardinal

Planet: Saturn

SUPERPOWER: THE POWER TO STRATEGIZE

You're ambitious, complicated, and hard to read. If I'm making you sound serious, it's because you are! But of course you have an earthy vibe, a strong libido, and a wry sense of humor. Money, success, and respect are important to you, and you often judge yourself too harshly. You were born old and are said to grow younger as you age—on the outside and the inside. Your superhero identity of the Planner is always looking to come up with the smartest road map before journeying forward with any goal.

On the inside you tend to see yourself as a mogul or the GOAT in your field. Your eye is always on the long-term prize. Making moves on impulse is not your style, while "picturing the end and working backward" certainly is. What's tricky is that the world is radically changing, and long-term plans aren't what they used to be! The Pluto in Aquarius era is all about chaos, change, and progress.

However, you have a superpower that was made for this kind of world: the power to strategize. Planning and putting the pieces of the puzzle together turn you on. And with the world as it is, we need you badly! As chaos rules the day, you are able to pull what was useful from the old paradigms and mix them with what's brand-new to get the job done. Whether the job is helping the environment, bringing new technology to the public, or introducing new forms of government when the old ones have failed, you are the one to get it done.

Famous Capricorns like Timothée Chalamet, Lin-Manuel Miranda, Muhammad Ali, and Dolly Parton are all ambitious and multifaceted. Chalamet spent five years preparing to play Bob Dylan. Miranda changed theater history with *Hamilton*. Ali fought to win not just in the boxing ring but also on the streets for civil rights. And Parton started in poverty and became a huge country star, actress, *and* philanthropist. Her father never learned how to read, and she poured millions and millions into books for children's libraries. Capricorns, you have soul and you never forget where you came from. Your superhero identity is the Planner, and you are fine with using strategy to achieve your goals slowly but steadily. That said, once you excel in your field, you never forget who helped you land where you are.

SUPERPARTNER POWER

You enjoy stability, preferably with a partner you can be proud of. Your career and personal life tend to overlap, so you may like it if whomever you are with elevates your public standing. In relationships, be they romantic or platonic, work can sometimes be the glue that holds it all together.

When you are not going out to network, you also love to use your skills as the Planner to come up with fabulous vacations or projects you and your honey can do together. As a partner, you tend to be the "teamwork makes the dreamwork" type. Whether it's renovating a space, taking an adventurous trip, or creating a start-up together, you love to collab with the one you love.

However, you are not all work and no play. You are surprisingly libidinous. I say surprisingly because you likely don't lead with that. But you are more rough and ready than you look! You have the power to dominate or be dominated, and whichever role you're playing, you go all in. For someone who is so direct and mature, you really can throw yourself into role-play! So you dig working hard, getting down and dirty, and going on vacay with your boo.

But that's not all!

Your ability to strategize is really a gift when it comes to long-term relationships. Real life is full of curveballs, especially in this unpredictable era. Your down-to-earth smarts and ability to handle problems with maturity can really make your partner feel like they have an ally.

SUPERCOMMUNITY POWER

Any community is lucky to have you, Capricorn. I mean, your superhero identity is the Planner and you possess the power to strategize! Yes, you can sometimes be aggressive and impatient while working on a task, but your skills and work ethic are so phenomenal, who cares? Besides, you only get impatient with people who sit there talking about talking rather than getting down to business. Delegating is another great skill of yours, as is staying power.

As a friend, you are patient, compassionate, and practical. You support your buds in times of need and are one of the most reliable people a friend can turn to. Okay, so you can be a little cheap sometimes. It's possible that your fastidious bookkeeping and check-splitting makes your friends laugh, especially if you follow your inclination to be exact down to the cent. You have a fabulous sense of humor and great comic timing, but being a cheapskate may be your blind spot!

SUPERSHADOW

As much as you love and protect your friends and show integrity in your work, you do have a mercenary streak, Capricorn. When it comes to money and prestige, you want to be number one. And if you occasionally throw someone under the bus to get what you want, well, you may chalk it up to the price of doing business. Now, keep in mind, this is not an everyday occurrence. It's more important to think about the rare occasions when you have allowed greed or ambition to blind you and think about how you would act if you could do it over again.

If this is not resonating for you, think about Macbeth. His fatal flaw was ambition, but it was Lady Macbeth who acted in the most mercenary way. Perhaps you have been able to skate through morally dicey situations with your hands clean, but ask yourself: Have you allowed someone else to be the bad guy in your stead?

The other way this shadow trait may play out is through resentment. Perhaps you sit on your high horse, afraid to go for what you want, and then resent those who've done as you wish you had the guts to. It's very human, Capricorn. We all have flaws, and we all act in ways that we might describe as "not our finest moment." So don't sweat it. But do meditate on the type of incidents that trigger strong feelings around mercenary behavior, times when you've put your own interests first at the cost of a relationship or your ethics. What motivated you? What were you afraid of? Once you uncover the answers to these questions, the shadow will fade.

SUPERFOES

THE CLOSE-MINDED MONSTER AND DEBBIE DOWNER

It is sometimes hard for you to accept someone else's worldview. You love to describe yourself as skeptical, but sometimes you shut down every idea that doesn't align with your own way of seeing things. When the Close-Minded Monster rears her righteous head, she is ready to put anyone down for offering an alternative point of view. Capricorn, if you can hear yourself demeaning someone in a mocking voice, cease and desist immediately!

As for Debbie Downer, well . . . you are a serious sort and you can worry a lot. In fact, you may even worry when there is nothing to worry about. This pessimistic vibe can be a real buzzkill! The key to dealing with this foe is moderation. Don't allow yourself to go on too many downward spirals in a day, a week, or a month. Keep track of your depressing responses! Cut down on them like you would cigarettes or sugar (two more things to worry about)!

Tarot

Capricorn is a sign that prefers the difficult truth over delusions that tick like time bombs. When it comes to loaded subjects, they are adept at taking a somewhat lawyerly approach and laying cards on the table, being honest about issues that most people avoid.

Capricorn is associated with the ninth major arcana card, the Devil. When reading cards, I tend to associate the Devil with taboo sex and divorce. Yes, it's rather extreme!

When it comes up in a spread, it usually indicates something that is societally frowned upon is causing the querent shame and distress. Interestingly, that doesn't mean the obvious sort of thing. It could refer to a queer man who is suddenly interested in a woman. As for divorce, I see this because if a person sublimates their true nature to make a relationship work, it is likely they are in the wrong relationship. However, if each person in the relationship brings their *devils* out into the open, the union can become transcendent —and this is what you are good at, Capricorn. In the Rider-Waite tarot deck, two lovers, reminiscent of the pair from the Lovers card, are now chained together and wearing horns. Break the chains of love with your radical honesty!

Kabbalah

ע

In the ancient mystical system of Kabbalah, Capricorn is connected to the sixteenth primordial Hebrew letter, ayin. *Ayin* translates to "eye" and refers to the ability to see, but not just using our visual sense. It means to really see, beyond just the obvious. Capricorn, earthy as you may be, you are also full of soul, and when you open your third eye to allow intuition to come through—and when you open up your heart chakra so you can truly "see" the person, plant, or planet right in front of you—you ascend to a higher level of living.

On the Kabbalistic Tree of Life, Capricorn travels the path between Tiferet, the sphere of beauty and harmony, and Hod, the sphere of divine judgment and prophecy. To enjoy the earthly delights and beauty of human life, one must use one's deepest ability to "see" what is real and true. Even though it's a rare Capricorn who would call himself a prophet, as your tribe tends to be much more no-nonsense, you do have an uncanny ability to see the truth.

In Kabbalah, Capricorn is associated with the month of Tevet. Tevet connects to Capricorn's astrological ruler, Saturn, the planet of hard work and discipline. But when the work is done, remember that Tevet is also a celebratory month. Hanukkah, the Festival of Lights, spends its first two nights in Tevet. Let there be light!

Your Magic Spell

When you have forgotten you are more than just human—you are a superhero of the infinite—use this magic spell:

Use your fingers to draw a map in the soil, the grass, or the sand (or use your imagination to do so), and say aloud or silently to yourself:

"I am a Planner. I strategize the best steps forward for myself and the world.

Universe, what is the most efficient path for me to take?"

THE THREE SUPERDECANATES OF CAPRICORN

First-Decanate Capricorn:

The Saturn/Cardinal Decanate

Sun in Capricorn 0 Degrees to 9 Degrees

Approximately December 22 to December 31

You folks are the Capricorniest of the Capricorns! Practicality rules where you are concerned. Being close to nature brings out the best in you and mirrors one of your greatest qualities: patience. Money means a lot to you, even though you wear your cards close to the vest in that area. Chances are, you will be the most successful the older you get. You always look at the long game. Just make sure you treat yourself with the utmost respect. Sometimes you seek it out from other people (who really *do* respect you) when what you need is to treat yourself with dignity.

Upcoming Outer Planet Transits

Pluto will be nudging your Sun through January 2032, to release the dead wood in your life and in your belief system. The more you can do this the happier you will be. You hate to give up, but letting go of projects, people, and self-concepts that no longer serve you will make room for a glorious new era in your life. In particular, focus on letting go and reinventing in the financial area of your life.

Second-Decanate Capricorn:

The Venus/Fixed Decanate

Sun in Capricorn 10 Degrees to 19 Degrees

Approximately January 1 to January 10

Middle-decanate Capricorns tend to be the most romantic. The Venus influence really softens you up and makes you prioritize love and pleasure over career and cash. The fixed influence also suggests that once you are committed, you stay committed. Venus, by way of fellow earth sign Taurus, also brings you artistic gifts, often with music and cooking. Having your home be a peaceful place is the key to your happiness. Tensions and fighting are hard for you to take. You need a pleasing environment with mood lighting, quality textures to touch, and home-loving people beside you.

Upcoming Outer Planet Transits

Dreamy and sometimes illusory Neptune will be aspecting your Sun between May 2028 and March 2036. You tend to be a little more passive than the average Capricorn and fear making wrong moves. But you have the gift of heightened intuition during this cycle and should take advantage. Literally ask the universe for help. It will answer. The key is in forming clear questions and being okay with any answer.

Third-Decanate Capricorn:

The Mercury/Mutable Decanate

Sun in Capricorn 20 Degrees to 29 Degrees

Approximately January 11 to January 20

Late-decanate Capricorns are influenced by Mercury, the planet of communication, and tend to be the brightest and brainiest of the bunch. Ideas and language are your forte, and you love to dig into deep, intellectual convos. Having a mutable influence over you gives you more flexibility than the usual Capricorn. You don't necessarily want to adapt, but you are able to. And part of you welcomes mixing up your routines a bit, even if you complain at first. Putting your feelings into words in a journal can help you better understand your dark places.

Upcoming Outer Planet Transits

Uranus in Gemini aspects your Sun between August 2029 and August 2032. Uranus is full of surprises and invites you to focus on the future and how bright it can be. Gemini is ruled by Mercury and is egging you on to put your message out into the world and help people who see the world a little differently come together and create a better way of life. When in doubt, follow your sense of humor and frivolity.

❋ YOUR MERCURY SUPER SIDEKICK ❋

Capricorn Sun with Mercury in Capricorn: This placement gives you an especially salty sense of humor and a sexy voice. Double the Capricorn influence also means double the shoptalk, so be sure to mix it up a little. You don't have to resort to talking about the weather, but at least stay up-to-date on your friends' lives and what's going on in pop culture.

Capricorn Sun with Mercury in Sagittarius: You tend to be a little less somber than the average Capricorn and more expansive in your world view. Since Sagittarius is the Traveler, it would be lucky for you to learn other languages. You never know when you may travel to a faraway land!

Capricorn Sun with Mercury in Aquarius: The influence of Aquarius makes you highly intellectual and very ahead of your time. Although you treat everyone like a friend, which is lovely, you also sometimes talk like a robot. Humanize your speech for the peeps, Capricorn.

Aquarius the Visionary

January 20 to February 18

Element: Air

Mode: Fixed

Planet: Uranus

SUPERPOWER: THE POWER TO INVENT

Aquarius, have you always felt as if you are an alien who has mysteriously landed on planet Earth? You likely have always felt that the world, and in particular the *humans* in the world, simply don't make sense. A bit like *Star Trek*'s Mr. Spock, you are here to promote peace and exploration even if you don't understand the species you have been thrown in with.

Luckily, your time is here, Aquarius! Your superhero identity is that of the Visionary, your superpower, the power to invent. During this Pluto in Aquarius era, which lasts until 2044, the universe will be reinventing itself, and we will be lucky if you lead the way. As a Visionary, you are more connected to the future than the past. And as an inventor, you are always using the present to create the future.

Ruled by Uranus, the planet of abrupt change, you see opportunity to make the world a better place when others are holding on bare-knuckled to a past that is already fading. You are consistent in character, with a humanitarian streak and the identity of a true friend. However, you can change course on a dime when you see a chance to help the species (or a small sector of it) evolve.

Rather than complain about what can't be changed, you tend to move decisively toward the new with confidence and clarity, creating a better world rather than complaining about current troubles.

Like Scorpios, your sign can be divisive, with people fangirl or fanboying you or attacking your methods and message. Still, you change the world by following your own vision, so let the trolls do what they do. Aquarian Oprah Winfrey changed the way the culture communicated, Abraham Lincoln changed the way the country showed humanity, Mozart and Bob Marley each changed the course of music (if only they could have collabed!), Michael Jordan changed the world of basketball, and David Lynch changed cinema and television. Remember, Aquarius, you are the Visionary. You imagine what the world needs way before the rest of humanity catches on. So invent to your heart's content; the people will (eventually) follow.

✵ SUPERPARTNER POWER ✵

You prioritize friendship, and not just with your platonic buds. It's also important to you that your romantic partners are your close friends too. The same way your friends can say anything to you and you won't judge, so too your lovers and partners can authentically be themselves. At the same time, you need a lot of space to think deep, cerebral thoughts, experiment like a mad scientist, and geek out in full nerd regalia. If your partner can retreat to their own space or do their own thing while you are doing yours, great! If your partner is needy and likes to talk about the relationship a lot, you may rub each other the wrong way.

Speaking of rubbing . . .

Sexually, you love to experiment. Being kinky may even be such a part of your identity that the most transgressive thing you could do is go vanilla! Some of you were made for threesomes or moresomes, as you may not be prone to jealousy, and you enjoy a group experience and the chance to make new friends. (Have you heard of book clubs?)

Being weird and eccentric is just part of your fabulousness, and your odd take on the world and Visionary ability to see the future will inspire partners to let *their* freak fly! You are also the most likely of the twelve signs to be a nudist. (Applause, please.) So if you are with someone who is also comfortable with their body, that will work nicely.

Mainly, you don't see your partner or friends as your possession. If people change and grow, that's great in your view. Even if they grow away from you temporarily, you know that giving them a choice ensures they will come closer again.

Intimacy may not be your forte, but you are very likely to create, with your honey, a different kind of relationship, one that doesn't abide by the rules of the conventional world. You're an optimist, after all!

✵ SUPERCOMMUNITY POWER ✵

You are a great friend and community member who prioritizes platonic relationships and being part of a values-aligned group. Being detached and committed is a powerful combo. You have the ability to view your friend group, your community organizations, your neighborhood with a wide-angle lens to really see any of these groups as a whole. Rather than sticking to old rules, you are great at infusing new energy into groups. Reinvention is your jam. Your very presence adds an electric energy to any discussion. You are an idea person and excellent at brainstorming. Since you operate well as a collaborator, you are not threatened by other people's brilliance. In fact, you encourage your friends and colleagues to shine.

Your sign is closely associated with technology, so you are apt to be the one who brings your brethren into the future. Change is going to be part of our everyday lives like never before. Your team members and allies are lucky to have you and your mad Visionary skills.

✵ SUPERSHADOW ✵

You can hold people at a distance without even realizing it. That's okay. You are just learning how to be human, after all! The shadowy part happens when you deny other people's reality. Rather than being vulnerable and saying something like, "Often I struggle to communicate emotionally," which would open the door for more conversation and a more honest discussion, you tend to revert to more distance.

Rather than retreat into your own head, it would behoove you to open up your heart a little more. First connect with yourself. If you can allow your heart to have a voice, not just your intellect, that would be a fine start. You may not understand the difference between thoughts and feelings. That's okay, as it gives you a chance to do some self-inquiry with a "don't-know mind" and truly befriend yourself. When you get to know some of your fears and resentments, and accept them as just part of your experience, then you can move forward in your relationships.

Although you are nonjudgmental about people's actions, it's their feelings that somehow befuddle you and even make you mad. This may lead to a tendency to distance yourself. But if you were to work toward accepting all the colors of your own emotional rainbow, you might find that you have anger to release. You may feel that getting angry is beneath you, but again, it's just normal. I know being normal is the last thing you want to be! But if you want to be relational, you need to at least understand the basics.

Once you wade through some of your own feelings, then you can really connect emotionally. Think of it like a foreign character you are embodying in a role-playing game! Find a way to make the part your own.

SUPERFOES

THE PUBLIC DEITY AND CONDESCEND-INATOR

The Public Deity is the part of you that is an absolutely warm and loving version of yourself, and it comes out when you are dealing with people you barely know. The public likely sees you as possessing a great deal of goodwill and a high EQ. Yet when you go home you act like a cold beeyatch to your besties. What's that about? Be careful of the Public Deity because, without realizing it, you can turn into a real Dr. Jackass and Mr. Hide-Your-Real-Self. You are so smart; can't you apply the skills you use in public to your personal relationships? A good way to fight this monster is to remind yourself of how much you love the people you are close to. Try a simple trick like setting an alarm with a song that makes you feel all warm and fuzzy for when the workday is done. This could be a cue to shift into your personal life and do so with sweetness.

The Condescend-inator sits on a high horse and looks down upon any intellectual point of view that seems "irrational" or lacking a "knowledge base." In other words, you can be a real know-it-all. How about experimenting like the true Visionary you are and seeing what you can learn from other people's points of view?

MYSTICAL SUPERPOWERS

Tarot

Aquarius is associated with the seventeenth major arcana card, the Star. In the Rider-Waite tarot deck, the Star is painted as a nude woman pouring water into water. Behind her we see a beautiful blue skyscape suggestive of the heavens. There is an openness and optimism to the Star. What would life be like if each of us followed our "North Star" and did the thing we came here to do? Aquarians are the sign most likely to be nudists, as I mentioned before, and here we see a figure who has none of the typical body shame. She is openly herself and believes everyone should be just as free. As the Visionary, you do not ask "Why?" but rather "Why not?"

Rabbalah

צ

In the ancient practice of Kabbalah, Aquarius is associated with the eighteenth primordial letter in the Hebrew alphabet, tzadik. A tzadik is also a figure who does good deeds in secret. I can't think of anything more Aquarian! When one is tormented inside, depression can lift when the focus is shifted to helping another. Aquarius knows this and practices this regularly. We all should!

On the Kabbalistic Tree of Life, Aquarius travels the path between Tipharet and Chokmah. Tipharet represents beauty and harmony, while Chokmah represents wisdom. I think of this path as a lesson in putting wisdom before beauty. When inner knowledge is given priority, only then can we see real beauty, not just the superficial kind.

Aquarius is associated with the Kabbalistic month of Shevat. Shevat marks a time for us to assess our environment, look at what is dying (in winter), and work toward the renewal of spring. In this Pluto in Aquarius age, we have no more time to take the environment for granted, and in true Visionary fashion we are called upon to use even times of dying to make sure that the dying is not in vain. We can build new growth.

Your Magic Spell

When you have forgotten you are more than just human—you are a superhero of the infinite—use this magic spell:

Use your fingers to draw invisible symbols in the air (or use your imagination), and say aloud or silently to yourself:

"I am a Visionary. I invent new systems to advance myself and the world.

Universe, what is the most leading-edge path for me to take?"

THE THREE SUPERDECANATES OF AQUARIUS

First-Decanate Aquarius:

The Uranus/Fixed Decanate

Sun in Aquarius 0 Degrees to 9 Degrees

Approximately January 19 to January 29

Early-decanate Aquarians like to stir up good trouble. They don't like to play by the rules, as independence is of prime importance to them. Disruptive Uranus affects them doubly, meaning they can stir up change in their own lives for reasons that are a mystery to them. Putting energy into worthy causes—perhaps inventing new kinds of relationships or new kinds of businesses—is the best way for these extravisionary folks to find peace of mind. But there is always a part of them that wants to use their intellect in ways that no human has ever done before.

Upcoming Outer Planet Transits

Pluto in Aquarius will be transiting your Sun through April 2030, inspiring you to reinvent yourself. When you were a child, what did you want to be? What drives you? Ask yourself the big questions, and don't be afraid to take a leap of faith. The world needs you now more than ever, and beyond 2030 there is a long cycle of Pluto in Aquarius (through 2044) when the world could truly benefit from your Visionary talents. Invent something new that helps humanity evolve.

In addition, Uranus will be making a benevolent trine aspect to your Sun through July 2028. This is another indication that you need to put your mind to dreaming up an idea that allows new systems to emerge, new paradigms, and shows humanity we can be less violent and more brilliant than in centuries past.

Second-Decanate Aquarius:

The Mercury/Mutable Decanate

Sun in Aquarius 10 Degrees to 19 Degrees

Approximately January 30 to February 8

Gifted at languages and communication in all forms, these Aquarians relish leading the life of the mind. The influence of Mercury makes them lighthearted and funny, and fun in social situations. That said, they don't like to go too deep unless it's into something that involves theory. They enjoy flitting from idea to idea and making new friends with like-minded glorious geeks. Of all Aquarians, middle-decanate Visionaries are the most spontaneous. They tend to slip into magical new eras in their lives by accident, just by connecting randomly with the most unexpected people.

Upcoming Outer Planet Transits

Uranus in Mercury-ruled Gemini will be forming a smooth trine to your Sun between July 2027 and June 2031. During this cycle, it would be wise of you to articulate what kind of change you want to see in the world and how you can be the change you wish to see. Pluto in Aquarius will be transiting your Sun between mid-January 2029 and mid-January 2039, encouraging you to rethink your worldly identity. If you decide to change vocations or invent a new way to live, trust that your instincts are right. You have always been ahead of your time, but during this period you are likely to be in sync with your time.

Third-Decanate Aquarius:

The Venus/Cardinal Decanate

Sun in Aquarius 20 Degrees to 29 Degrees

Approximately February 9 to February 18/19

Late-decanate Aquarians have a real romantic streak. The influence of Venus makes them partner-oriented, and they do well with a mate by their side. They are also likely to have strong artistic talents and a gift for aesthetics. They are apt to express themselves in surprising ways. Creativity gets them through difficult periods in life, as does immersing themselves in culture—both high and low. They think in metaphors and may not be the most direct communicators, but their hearts are in the right place.

Upcoming Outer Planet Transits

Pluto will be transiting your Sun between April 2034 and early March 2044. It's a time when you will be called to help your family, your peers, and society as a whole make sense of the massive changes in the world. Let your intellectual courage be your guide.

Overlapping with this cycle, Neptune, the planet of healing and imagination, will be in the cardinal sign of Aries and bringing you its spirit of initiative most strongly between mid-April 2033 and late March 2039. This is a long cycle in which you will be greatly valued as a real leader in the healing field as well as in the arts. Be the inspiration the world needs.

YOUR MERCURY SUPER SIDEKICK

Aquarius Sun with Mercury in Aquarius: You are the most logical communicator, and you tend to be the friendliest of the three Mercuries. You enjoy intellectual debates, but always have an eye on making new friends and expanding your posse.

Aquarius Sun with Mercury in Capricorn: You're likely to be more down-to-earth than most Aquarians, and you have a sexy voice and way of making your point. Body language is part of how you communicate. You have a strong sense of how to read the room and come up with practical ways to communicate.

Aquarius Sun with Mercury in Pisces: Your vibe is softer, and you are the most humanitarian of the bunch. There is a musicality to your speech, and you possess a little more telepathy than the average Aquarius. The Pisces influence helps you tune in to other people's frequencies and communicate on their level.

Pisces the Dreamer

February 19 to March 20

Element: Water

Mode: Mutable

Planet: Neptune

SUPERPOWER: THE POWER TO IMAGINE

How fascinating it would be to live inside your head, Pisces! Even the artists among you who put your dreams onto the page or the stage still hold a lot back, and boy is it wild! As a mutable sign, you change your tune from time to time, sometimes intuiting that a piece of your childhood you left behind needs to reemerge in a new form. Maybe you go from being a mathematician to being a musician or vice versa.

As the last sign of the zodiac, you internalize all the signs who came before you. You hold the whole astrological rainbow in your soul. This gives you a deep sense of empathy. Even if you haven't directly gone through what other signs have, you can *imagine*. You are also gifted with the power to heal. Perhaps you are in a helping profession or you are just a born healer. Do people ever tell you that they just feel better when they are around you? Well, there you go.

For a water sign, you are often said to spend a lot of time with your head in the clouds. And that's a good thing! After all, as above so below. You may fantasize about magical lands and a healthy planet, and then bring those visions down to earth. Pisces, you are a dreamer who uses the power of imagination to bring your dreams to life. So pay attention to what you dream up. During our times of chaos and surprise, you really could see those wishes come to fruition, so think them through. In Ursula Le Guin's science fiction novella, *The Lathe of Heaven*, the protagonist is blessed and cursed with the ability to dream up things that then become real. In trying to wield this power with good conscience, he dreams of a world where there are no racial divides. Everyone is the same. In the dream, everyone is gray. It's pretty dull and homogenized. So before you get too utopian about the world or your own life, use your heart and your mind to see things clearly.

Big-dreaming Pisceans include Olympian Simone Biles, actor and icon Drew Barrymore, legendary musicians Johnny Cash and Kurt Cobain, and last but not least, genius Albert Einstein, who recognized the mystical in the cosmos and sought to bring the mystery of the cosmos down to earth.

You Pisceans are known less for your logic and more for your imagination. Dreams don't always "make sense," but they can sometimes come true. And by believing in what's possible, you make dreams come true.

✵ SUPERPARTNER POWER ✵

You may appear sphinxlike on the outside and even come off a bit chilly. But once you have gotten pooky-wooky and cuddly-wuddly with your bae, you are as lovey as they come. You don't need to be taken care of, but let's face it, you do love it! There is something childlike about you that brings out the caretaker in your mate. Of course you are a caretaker yourself, but in ways that tend to be more ethereal and hard to quantify.

Once you are in a relationship you still maintain an active fantasy life. Sometimes you share with your partner, sometimes you don't. Your vibe veers toward superpassionate. Unless you are going through a self-loathing phase, in which case your doors are temporarily shut. You do have a tendency to get into trouble when your imagination gets the better of you and veers over the line into obsession. Platonic friends know how to snap you back to reality, usually by getting you excited about a creative project or letting you cry it out over a movie. In relationships, you Pisceans do stir up some drama, but it's only because your moods can be confusing—even to you.

You are an excellent gift giver, and you freely offer tea and sympathy to friends and lovers when they need it most. But sometimes it's hard for you to articulate your own needs. This can lead to resentments building up, so make sure you give your partners a chance to understand your feelings.

Sometimes you like to immerse all your energy into your partner, but you might not want them to be too clingy with you. And sometimes you require the reverse. You are a mystery wrapped up in a riddle tied up with an enigmatic bow!

✵ SUPERCOMMUNITY POWER ✵

You love being part of a posse. Sometimes you get teary just sitting at a table and looking at your buds and allies, wondering how you all found each other. Your wit and whimsy come out when you are hanging in a group. Since you spend so much time in your head, it helps to have real people to engage with.

When it comes to serving your community, you are right there ready to give it your all. But sometimes you promise too much. Get a handle on what's realistic for you to give. Your heart breaks when you see injustice, or sometimes a rare show of temper bursts free. But it is hard for you to not contribute your energy when you witness suffering.

When it comes to friends, you sometimes get all crushy. There is something about the intimacy and affection you share with a pal that turns your head to romance. You may be a poly Pisces, but chances are it's your unavailable buddies you swoon over. It's pretty harmless, and you can always put your yearning into a love ballad. Everybody wins!

✵ SUPERSHADOW ✵

You're delightful, you're delicious, and sometimes you are bloody de-lu-lu! Yes, you can fall into delusional states and become detached from reality. But we all have faults! On the one hand, your friends and loved ones may find these brief periods when you go completely off the rails to be funny and charming. On the other hand, it can get old fast.

In Tennessee Williams's classic drama, *A Streetcar Named Desire*, Blanche must have been a Pisces. After all, one of her quotable lines is: "I don't want realism. I want magic!" She prefers the gauzy illusion of a paper lantern to the stark illumination of truth. "I can't stand a naked light bulb, any more than I can a rude remark or a vulgar action." Yes, your rules and reactions are dramatic, but when they cross the line into extreme, it becomes a problem.

Rather than push your shadow away or get defensive about it, try engaging with it. Ask that part of you that turns your life into an over-the-top opera what she needs. My guess is attention. She has spent so much time building up secret worlds that when she starts acting them out, she has trouble distinguishing fantasy from reality. Perhaps what Delulu You needs from Stable You is your undivided attention. Then she won't have to try so hard to get it.

✵ SUPERFOES ✵

THE VAGUE VILLAIN AND THE VILLAINOUS VICTIM

The Vague Villain is recognizable by the glazed look in his eyes. He spaces out and doesn't seem to know if the person in front of him is alive or an inanimate object. For that matter, he may not know if he himself is alive or frozen in time. The Vague Villain's evil super power is the ability to gaslight. He will act as if he doesn't understand what's going on. He may say, "You never said that" or "I never did that. You did." When he's confronted with evidence, he spaces out even more. Beware the empty eyes! A good way to snap this monster out of it is to give yourself a pinch! This cue may bring a tear to your eyes, but then you will be back in your emotions, not completely turned off to human connection. Remind him he has beautiful eyes, a beautiful expressiveness, and he should strive to be a hero, not a villain!

The Villainous Victim is a cousin to the Vague Villain. She loves playing the world's smallest violin and putting on her best victim-y cosplay garb. Being the victim is more fun to her than a day at the beach. But you know what she enjoys the most? Gathering up your mutual friends and repeating the excruciating and manipulated details of how she has been wronged. You are probably going to take her side because of the tears pooling in her eyes. But be careful—you may her next . . . er . . . victim.

To combat this V. V., use a little reverse psychology and say, "You are strong and powerful. You are not a victim."

MYSTICAL SUPERPOWERS

Tarot

Pisces is represented by the eighteenth major arcana card in the tarot, the Moon. The Moon is a very poignant card. In the classic Rider-Waite tarot deck, the image is of a dog and a wolf howling at the moon. The dog represents our more domesticated nature, while the wolf signifies the wild animal instincts that also live within. Often when this card arises it makes me think of star-crossed love. Perhaps you are in love with someone who lives on another continent. Their home is in Africa. Yours in the United States. They cannot leave their home; you cannot leave yours. It is best to accept the mysterious forces of the universe and trust there is a greater plan. What a Pisces operatic tale! Somehow life goes on, though, and sadness allows us to recognize joy.

Kabbalah

ק

In the ancient mystical tradition of Kabbalah, Pisces is connected to the nineteenth primordial letter in the Hebrew alphabet, kuf. Kuf is a letter of endings and new beginnings, much like the twelfth house is in the astrological chart. (The house that Pisces rules.) There is a bittersweet melancholy to saying goodbye and moving on, but great excitement at the prospect of starting fresh.

Pisces is associated with the Moon Path on the Kabbalistic Tree of Life. This falls between the bottom sefirot, Malchut, representing the material world, and Netzach, which symbolizes victory through faith. Being a Pisces sometimes means feeling in this world but not of it. Yet by keeping the faith, whatever that means for you, victory is assured.

The month associated with Pisces on the Hebrew calendar is the month of Adar, associated with miracles and wonder. Heavy as the Pisces experience can be, it is also capable of the greatest happiness.

Your Magic Spell

When you have forgotten you are more than just human—you are a superhero of the infinite—use this magic spell:

Use your fingers to place drops of water over your third eye (or use your imagination), and say aloud or silently to yourself:

"I am a Dreamer. I imagine healing myself and the world with love.

Universe, what is the most sensitive path for me to take?"

THE THREE SUPERDECANATES OF PISCES

First-Decanate Pisces:

The Neptune/Mutable Decanate

Sun in Pisces 0 Degrees to 9 Degrees

Approximately February 18/19 to February 28/29

Early-decanate Pisces are born with a double dose of Neptune and of mutability. The most Piscean of the lot, they excel when they use artistic outlets to express themselves. They may seem withdrawn, but it's really just shyness. Their intuition is strong, and many can tap into their psychic powers through dreams, meditation, or by playing with the tarot and other divination tools. They have the innate ability to heal the wounds of their loved ones.

Upcoming Outer Planet Transits

Neptune will be pleasantly triggering your Sun through March 2031, and if ever there was a cycle to make your dreams of abundance and prosperity come true, this would be the time. The transit affects your solar house of money and property. Become friends with money. Let go of any resentments or guilt about your past relationship. Financial paradigms are changing, and you need to move forward as well.

Over the same period and a little bit beyond (through January 2032), Pluto will be encouraging you to let go of what no longer serves you so that you can make room for new and better things in your emotional and spiritual life.

Second-Decanate Pisces:

The Lunar/Cardinal Decanate

Sun in Pisces 10 Degrees to 19 Degrees

Approximately March 1 to March 10

Middle-decanate Pisceans are great in the kitchen, and keeping their domicile lovely is important to them, as is family (bio and/or chosen). The influence of the Moon makes them especially moody, but luckily the lunar cycle also contributes to the predictability of their moods. Making everyone feel like family is important to them. They are likely to have intense relationships with their mom. You know they love you if they give you a key to their hut or invite you to the beach.

Upcoming Outer Planet Transits

From May 2028 through May 2031, Uranus, the planet of sudden change and progress, will be aspecting your Sun. As a result, you may feel like pulling up stakes and moving or taking your career in a different direction. You may be craving a more exciting life. Just remember that it starts with how much you are leading the life of the mind. You could have a real yearning to learn and to invent. Let yourself explore and experiment on yourself first, before you make more literal moves.

Third-Decanate Pisces:

The Pluto/Fixed Decanate

Sun in Pisces 20 Degrees to 29 Degrees

Approximately March 11 to March 20/21

Pluto's intense and highly sexual influence makes these Pisceans more erotically curious and prone to turbulence. That said, they can use their experiences to understand themselves better. They dive deep, even if sometimes the waters scare them. The fixed energy makes them more reliable and apt to stick with projects and people for a long time. They tend to be long-range thinkers. Some may be prone to addiction, but what they really need is to nurture themselves and turn self-loathing into self-love. They have the ability to make themselves seem invisible, and then they'll spring up when you least expect it!

Upcoming Outer Planet Transits

Uranus sparks some new energy in your home and family sector between mid-August 2029 and late May 2038. Don't just settle for a house you like. Go for your dream home. The same holds true for family dynamics. You don't need to follow traditional rules. Experiment!

Pluto will also be aspecting your Sun between March 2035 and March 2044. This is a time for you to allow the world to see the real you behind the persona. Pluto is concerned with depth and truth in human affairs. The more you show your flaws and past mistakes, the more your future is assured, as you will gain the public's trust. This is true in your personal life too.

YOUR MERCURY SUPER SIDEKICK

Pisces Sun with Mercury in Pisces: You communicate with wit and wisdom, and you prefer not to pin your ideas down too much. Rather than use dry facts to make your point, you prefer weaving together a spellbinding narrative.

Pisces Sun with Mercury in Aquarius: You can be quite brilliant when you are focusing on one of your passions. The words fly free, mixing futuristic ideas with data-driven evidence. The combo of Pisces with Aquarius is innately ahead of its time. People may not always understand what the hell you're talking about, but they will find you fascinating!

Pisces Sun with Mercury in Aries: You are the most direct, least vague of Pisceans. You take your imagination and focus it on something you want to bring to life in the real world. And you use succinct language as your secret weapon.

STEP THREE

Collab with Your Big-Three High-Vibe Tribe

NOW THAT YOU KNOW THE SUPERPOWERS YOU GET FROM your Sun sign, it's time to learn more about your Big Three. These include your Sun sign that rules the mind, your Moon sign that rules the heart, and your Rising sign that rules the body. You will learn how to consult your particular Big-Three High-Vibe Tribe and ask them for guidance. Now let's meet the contestants!

✵ SUN SIGN (YOUR MIND MATE) ✵

Your Sun sign is the member of your friend group who helps you come up with ideas and make decisions. Call upon this member of your High-Vibe Tribe when you need help using your mental faculties to make the right moves.

Aries Sun: I am here to help you make decisions and take action. Instead of worrying about the long term, I can help you deal with the here and now. Now let's think about what we can do the fastest and the soonest. If we use our minds, we can ascertain what it is that we want. As an Aries Sun I am proud to say, "I want what I want when I want it" (also the name of a mixtape I made in the '80s). Once we're clear on our desire, let's ask: Do we need it now, absolutely right now? If the answer is yes, then what's the first bold action step we can take? Don't be afraid; I'm not.

And remember, I am your Mind Mate. So let's try to detach for a moment and come up with a quick description of what we are going for and why. Okay, I'm getting bored with that too. How about we plug into how it will feel to be the winner in this battle. I know we might not technically be at war, but as Sun Tzu says in *The Art of War*: "He will win who knows when to fight and when not to fight." Our Warrior ways are always working for us, even when we are at rest. And if you are wondering how to use this sharp Aries mind of ours, remember our motto is "act first, think later." We possess an innate courage. We are ruled by Mars, the planet of passion, so when we feel an urge to jump, dagnabbit, we have to trust that impulse.

Converse with Your Mind on the Daily

Before you start your day, ask your mind:
How can I be my best Warrior self today?

Taurus Sun: Hello. I am here to show you how to move like an animal. Animals only take as many steps as they need to (not including your kitten King Krazy—he likes to zigzag as if his tail is on fire, then slide under the couch for no reason). But as your Mind Mate, I must advise you to move slowly. If you want to access the best of our Taurus mind, you need to look at a situation in the simplest terms. What is the essential question we should ask? If we were to describe this situation in the most straightforward terms without using fancy language, what would we say?

The best way to use your Taurus Mind Mate (a.k.a. me!) is to feel your way into what you are mulling over. When you feel a sense of fullness in your belly and a simple step comes to mind, you're in! Our sign is the Maker, and building is our superpower. Let's think about what exactly we need to build in this situation. What needs a solid foundation, and what's the first step we can take to build it? There's no rush. We take our time. And since we are ruled by Venus, beauty means a lot to us. Surely we can find a way to make what we build into a practical work of art.

Converse with Your Mind on the Daily
Before you start your day, ask your mind:
How can I be my best Maker self today?

Gemini Sun: I am so glad to be here for you as your Mind Mate! But let's get down to business quickly, before I get distracted. We are the sign of the Messenger, and we possess the power to communicate. We tend to work best by just brainstorming. Just say every little thought that comes to mind. Let's riff! Let's just have fun and see what happens. And you know, I'm totally cool with bringing in some pals to brainstorm too. Even if we're sitting on a plane, we can just ask the person next to us a random question. Through the powers of synchronicity we might receive a clue.

And after a short time, let's see if we stumble on a direction we need to take. Once we start moving toward a destination using our mind, we can ask ourselves why we are drawn there. But let's not get too heavy about it. The key to finding the answers we seek is through having fun, being in the moment, and not getting too attached to the outcome. If we don't solve our problem this very minute, it'll usually keep. In fact, sometimes doing something else we enjoy could put us back on the path, and then the answer comes when we're in the shower the next day!

Converse with Your Mind on the Daily
Before you start your day, ask your mind:
How can I be my best Messenger self today?

Cancer Sun: I know that we Cancers are known for being very emotional, but we are so much more than that. Let me tell you, honey, how we can make the most of this wise Cancer mind of ours. First, let's start with how we identify. We are the Guardians of the zodiac, and we possess the power to protect. Let's apply these truths to our current quandary. What exactly needs protecting? We may find the answer by asking that question and following up with a few "whys."

Or, since our gut is always so damn right-on, if something deep down tells us we are being *over*protective, let's follow that lead. Let's first ask ourselves *why* we are being so protective; what are we afraid of? Once we know the answer, we can put down the armor and give ourselves and others a break. If we think things through and we realize we don't have to offer any protection, we will undoubtedly feel lighter. And we may then see the direction to take without all that emotional baggage weighing us down.

Remember, too, that we are a cardinal sign, which makes us gifted at coming up with ideas, making decisions, and then moving forward based on that intel. Let's use that skill, chop-chop. We Cancers are moody, so if we are in the mood *now*, let's get going.

Even though when we feel like hiding—our motto is "Hell is other people"—we also have times when we relish connection. Let's try to ask ourselves how we can work *with* other people to get what we need.

Converse with Your Mind on the Daily

Before you start your day, ask your mind:
How can I be my best Guardian self today?

Leo Sun: Darling, we are so lucky to have been born under the sign of Leo! Our sign is known as the Leader, and we possess the power to inspire. So let's inspire ourselves, shall we? First of all, we need to decide: What is the big, glorious vision we are working toward? Once we can tune in to the situation we're in with theatricality and verve, we can bring our best selves to the role.

Of course, we are not just about fabulous costumes and compelling charisma. We can go deep too. What about this situation sparks a feeling of grand passion? How can we transmute that feeling into practical terms? Our sign has ruled many a movie director—Christopher Nolan, Stanley Kubrick, Greta Gerwig, and Alfred Hitchcock, just for starters. Let's try to see the whole cinematic story in our heads before we make any moves.

It helps to identify the plot. Classic plot structure is Act I: Boy Meets Girl. Act II: Boy Loses Girl. Act III: Boy Tries to Get Girl Back. (Don't worry about the genders, though. The boys may very well be in drag.) Anyway, we can determine which act we are in *now* and how we want to direct the narrative.

And since directors are the boss of everything, we can zoom back in to examine the details. What costumes, music, and sets will help tell our story? Thinking like this can tell us where we want to meet our lead actors to perform the scene at hand. Whether we decide to meet in the bedroom using candlelight or out in the woods during magic hour, just remember we are in charge. And . . . action!

Converse with Your Mind on the Daily

Before you start your day, ask your mind:
How can I be my best Leader self today?

Virgo Sun: We are known to be the sign of details, my good mate—the Gardeners of the zodiac. As such, we possess the power to cultivate. So the best way for me to help you help yourself is by bringing a thoughtful, critical eye to the tiny tasks at hand. A good one to start with is this one: Do we have the proper tools and ingredients to work with?

Our critical thinking skills are strong, as we are ruled by clever Mercury. So let's not waste time lying to ourselves about what's not working. Instead, let's honor and show humble gratitude for what *is* working for us in this situation. Then let's build on that foundation. Remember, to cultivate means to nurture and refine.

The nurturing part tends to be easier than you think. What do the small parts of the whole need to grow and come to life? What are the little things we can do to perfect what we have grown? And of course, growing and nurturing our garden is not something we do in one day. We may need to dedicate a season to this work. And we should know we are privileged to be in the position to be of service. I mean, we do tend to know everything, so we shouldn't hoard our helpful hints, right?

Converse with Your Mind on the Daily

Before you start your day, ask your mind:
How can I be my best Gardener self today?

Libra Sun: Beauty is more than skin deep. We were born under the sign of the Artist and are able to harmonize elements to create splendor. To get the most out of me, your Mind Mate, ask me the most superficial questions you can think of about your current situation. There might be tiny, elegant gestures I could suggest that will bring peace where before there was friction. Or perhaps I can offer up a third point of view, different from the one you are worried about and the one you are hoping for. There might be a balance between the two options that hits the sweet spot. And then we can all sit back and enjoy our porridge, Goldilocks!

To harmonize also suggests the ability to find the most lovely sounds that blend together. You'd be surprised how well matters can go and how many troubles can be sorted out when we get the players involved operating on the same frequency.

When in doubt, or while we're figuring out options, here's some guidance: Maintain a small smile on your face, a peaceful expression, and be as neutral as Switzerland. Everyone will feel you're on their side. And guess what? You are! When everyone wins, you will feel great relief.

We are ruled by the element of air, which is associated with logic and rationality. Therefore, it behooves us to try to understand everyone's point of view. And if times suddenly get superturbulent, just breathe deeply (air), dress pretty (Venus is our ruler), and keep your feet firmly planted in the middle ground.

Converse with Your Mind on the Daily

Before you start your day, ask your mind:
How can I be my best Artist self today?

Scorpio Sun: We are lucky to be born under the sign of Scorpio, as we possess an incredibly sharp mind. Nothing gets by us. Our animal instincts are as strong as our powers of observation. But as your Mind Mate, the onus is on me to play straight with you. Sometimes we are too smart for our own good!

When dealing with challenges, we have our Shamanistic powers to call upon, which can be otherworldly, unquantifiable, and quite magical. If our brilliant and foolproof strategies can help turn a tricky situation around, let's use those techniques. But if our gut says that's not the right path, then here's what we'll do:

We will ask the universe to help us access our highest, most noble self with the goal of transforming a tough trial into a victorious outcome for all.

I'm your Mind Mate, and I am behind you a million percent. I want you to know that having me on your side is like having the brain and verbal powers of a lawyer. A great lawyer can cut through red tape and corruption to achieve justice. But at other times, it might be better to use our brilliant way with language more like a rabbi, a priest . . . a shaman! In other words, we want to get to the spirit of the contract, not just the letter of the law. For example, if you are in the midst of a heated quarrel, ask yourself if you are fighting just because you want to win this point, or if you would prefer to give the other person the benefit of the doubt, especially if you already have goodwill between you. You feel me?

And finally, serious and intense as our sign can sometimes be, let's not forget our innate powers of hilarity! Humor is the great uniter, so let's use it, not lose it!

Converse with Your Mind on the Daily

Before you start your day, ask your mind:
How can I be my best Shaman self today?

Sagittarius Sun: Speaking of humor (see our predecessor Scorpio's last line), we are more fun than a barrel full of monkeys! As your Mind Mate, I can tell you that the ability to laugh at ourselves is incredibly disarming to whatever individual or group we may be dealing with!

But we are not just here to act the part of the clown. We are the sign of the Traveler, and we possess the power to explore. We tend to be more cultured and well read than people realize, and we may have seen a lot of the world. Therefore, we have the ability to use tricks and techniques we've learned through exploring many lands and reading about the rest. What might land wrong on a German's ears may sound like music to a Venezuelan's. *Verstehst du*? I mean . . . *comprende*? In this way, we can see many points of view and are able to connect with people from all walks of life.

Sure, sometimes we suffer from foot-in-mouth disease, but that's because we are honest to a fault. We are also truth seekers. Why not use our sincerity and transparency to gently discover what the people we meet hold dear? We can avoid stepping on too many toes, break bread together, come to an amenable solution, and then have a party afterward! Last one on the dance floor is a rotten egg!

Converse with Your Mind on the Daily

Before you start your day, ask your mind:
How can I be my best Traveler self today?

Capricorn Sun: I would advise taking the long view, whatever the situation is. We Capricorns are ruled by Saturn, which tends to make us cautious. We suss out whether we want to take action or bide our time. Some may call us conniving, but really, we just tend to be patient and smart.

Our sign is known as the Planner, and we possess the power

to strategize. So let's have fun breaking down the problem at hand. First, is it urgent? What level of importance are we talking about? If it can be back-burnered, great. If the state of affairs is code red, then okay, let's think of the most rational, prudent approach. I know people may accuse us of being cold, but it's just that we play our cards close to the vest.

We are street savvy and good at business. Remember that the definition of a successful negotiation is one in which both parties walk away having given up something. Compromise is a social lubricant too. Is there a way we can show good faith and make a small sacrifice—lose a battle—to win a war?

Compromise is worth it if we want to maintain good long-term relationships. I know this all sounds very "politic," but human dynamics are political by nature. I can help us win in the long run. (And "winning" here can look like anything we want it to—whether it really is a great business deal or whether it's just having a rollicking fun day with our besties.)

Converse with Your Mind on the Daily

Before you start your day, ask your mind:
How can I be my best Planner self today?

Aquarius Sun: We are ruled by air, the element of ideas and logic. We don't look at life through the lens of "I," but rather through the lens of "we." Not to sound too much like Mr. Spock or an AI bot, but there really is no such thing as a problem. Perhaps the conditions we are dealing with are challenged, but we have the brain power to find the best solution. We are futurists by nature. Remember that yesterday's magic is today's science.

Yes, I know humans are obsessed with emotions, but I'll let your Moon in Aquarius ally speak to that. Let's just operate on the level of mind. Who exactly is telling us that there are difficulties? Can we break them down one by one and see what the common factor is?

And once we ascertain that, let's see which solution is the simplest and most elegant. The solution to a math equation should not have leftover numbers, right? Perfection may be elusive, but it is possible and certainly worth working toward. And remember, we work well with friends and teammates, so let's get everyone onboard. We are the sign of the Visionary and we possess the power to invent. We are also the optimists of the zodiac. Let's get started!

And one final note: Even though the above may sound a bit clinical, we Aquarians wear the banner of "Weirdest person on the block!" with pride. Eccentricity is one of our strengths. So even though we use rationality to deal with issues, we usually bring some whackado flair to the table while we're at it!

Converse with Your Mind on the Daily

Before you start your day, ask your mind:
How can I be my best Visionary self today?

Pisces Sun: I am just so moved and touched that you want my support, my help, my friendship. That's why I'm crying! Generally, we Pisceans operate on an emotional level, but we know how to use our noggins too.

When faced with a difficult situation, we are very good at ascertaining the roles and the motivations of all the characters involved. It's important to not just apply dry logic to a conundrum, but to observe the people who are involved.

They are the variables, and we need to look beneath the surface. What is each person involved the most sensitive about? What do they worry about? What are they ashamed of?

We are the sign of the Dreamer, and we possess the power to imagine. So let's say this world, this life is all just a dream we conjured up. If that's the case, and we are dealing with a major roadblock in our career, we could analyze the situation as we would a nighttime dream. What would the symbolic meaning of each of the elements of this dream be? Swiss psychologist Carl Jung (who also wrote at length about astrology, synchronicity, and other mystical matters) had a technique for dream interpretation. You could write down the narrative of the dream, and for all the objects, people, and places, write down your first association.

Take the big CEO that no one has ever met but who controls your salary—maybe you associate him with a monster? And what about your salary? What's the first word or phrase you associate with it? Security, perhaps? When you are done writing out the narrative of your current dilemma, using your first associations rather than the literal characters and things, what do you come up with? What is the message of your dream? Just suspend disbelief for a moment and say what comes to mind. It can be fun!

Converse with Your Mind on the Daily

Before you start your day, ask your mind:
How can I be my best Dreamer self today?

❋ MOON SIGN (YOUR EMOTIONAL RESCUE BESTIE) ❋

Your Moon sign is the member of your friend group who helps your heart. Call upon this member of your High-Vibe Tribe when you are feeling confused about a relationship situation or when you are emotionally dysregulated (in other words, when you are freaking out).

Aries Moon: Call upon me when you need some attention! We Aries Moons are so full of ardor, we can get rather blue when others go about their business in a dry, ho-hum way. We feel best when the energy in the room is high. But if you are ever having trouble reading the room, ask for my help. Of course you feel bummed out if you aren't getting enough excitement back from others. Instead of letting your mood plunge, look into my eyes (in literal terms, look in the mirror!) and see the attention I am paying you. I will never be withholding.

And for those who say that your temper is too quick to flare up, I say let out your feelings with me. Sometimes the fuse gets lit when you are feeling vulnerable. I will never criticize you for getting a little riled up, especially because you are so quick to recover.

Remember this: When you are feeling impatient or ignored, you are probably not giving yourself enough sunshine. So let me warm you up. I also can't stand people who act cold and distant, and I would never act that way with you. All you have to do is remember that I'm here. Put your hand over your heart and feel me.

Finally, don't worry about anyone calling you selfish. You have the ability to focus on a project, a dream, a relationship with passion and courage. And others may just be jealous because you are a doer, not merely a talker. What you create for yourself will actually benefit your loved ones and the world. Imagine if everyone followed their highest excitement!

Converse with Your Heart

Check in on your mood state a few times a day. Ask your heart to identify the mood you are in and how you can use your Moon sign's superpower—the power to take action—to elevate your mood.

Taurus Moon: Call on me if people are getting impatient with your patience! We live in a world that operates at warp speed, and that's just not how we roll. So if you are being castigated for your slow-cooking vibes, know that I have your back and your heart.

After all, when others burn themselves out with frenzied energy, we will have conserved ours. And I am here in your heart, the first one to soothe you with sweet nothings. And speaking of nothing, what's wrong with doing a lot of it (a lot of nothing, that is)?

Many people in this world define themselves by what they do. We, like nature itself, are satisfied just *being*. We make a good role model. Still, because we never toot our own horn and we often are the last to cross the finish line, it's easy for people to overlook us. But one day they will look up at the tall building in the sky, or the money earned to care for all, or the relationship that has stood the test of time, and see that it's our ability to do less, and even make do on smaller portions when times are tough, that makes us so solid and secure.

And speaking of security, no matter how much you

worry about money, know that you are wise enough to make the right decisions, learn from mistakes, and weather any storm. I am here to remind you that money and material things are also here to be enjoyed. Indulge yourself. Ruled by Venus, you do love luxury, and a little of it now and again is good for your soul.

Converse with Your Heart

Check in on your mood state a few times a day. Ask your heart to identify the mood you are in and how you can use your Moon sign's superpower—the power to build—to elevate your mood.

Gemini Moon: I may be known more for thinking than feeling, but I have a sensitive side too. If you are ever feeling like the withdrawn introvert in you is getting hassled, please call upon me. After all, I may just want to sit and do my *New York Times* crossword puzzle in ink and not be bothered with other people and their intrusive emotions.

I mean, look at us, friend, we take care of ourselves—and sometimes it's hard for us to understand why other people don't seem to do the same. And then they may even take it out on us for ignoring them and blame us for being cold and unfeeling. It can be hard not to wish that we could just be appreciated for our own lack of neediness. Do we ever put heavy demands on people? No! That's not our way. So why can't our loved ones respect our boundaries and our desire to just think, zone out, geek out, or do whatever we want?

On the other hand, we love to socialize! It's important we

balance things out by letting our dear ones in, not shutting them out. The bottom line is that we are at our best when we take care of ourselves with some chill alone time to be in our own heads, but then go out and play with our mates!

Converse with Your Heart

Check in on your mood state a few times a day. Ask your heart to identify the mood you are in and how you can use your Moon sign's superpower—the power to communicate—to elevate your mood.

Cancer Moon: Our sign is ruled by the Moon, so we are more in touch with its cycles than anyone else. I am a big believer in keeping track of the movements of the Moon. Seriously, start with the new Moon and make a note in your calendar what kind of mood you are in that day. Then, when the Moon shifts into its next phase, make a note of that too. And so on and so forth for the whole month. You'd be surprised to see how predictable your moods are with the Moon's phases. That certainly doesn't mean you are predictable in a negative way. You move the way nature does: in tune with the environment above and below.

People may accuse us of being moody. And so what if they're right? If we're feeling sensitive and need to do some self-care, we'll go for it. We put a lot of energy into nurturing everyone else, so we should make sure we give ourselves the same amount of tender loving care, if not more.

And believe me, honey, I get it when you are feeling self-protective. After all, our sign's superhero identity is that of the Guardian. The Guardian's superpower is the ability to protect. Before you can shield anyone or anything else from harm, you need to make sure you take care of yourself. When you are coming from a place of emotional strength, you can do anything. Those stories about a mom lifting a car to save her baby are no joke!

Converse with Your Heart

Check in on your mood state a few times a day. Ask your heart to identify the mood you are in and how you can use your Moon sign's superpower—the power to protect—to elevate your mood.

Leo Moon: You have such a big heart, darling, and that is what should always lead you. I know you fear being "too much," but to hell with anyone who dares to call you "extra." Is your generosity extra? Is your warmth toward people near you and the world at large extra? No! So you do you. And I am here to help remind you who you are and what really matters.

Don't let anyone ever make you feel like you have to shrink who you are. And remember that the best way to do that is to applaud yourself every time you take a go-big-or-go-home attitude. You love big; just make sure you love yourself even bigger. And when you're feeling blue, doll yourself up, take a look in the mirror, and let your jaw drop in response to the beauty you see in that glass!

The arts are another way to lift your spirits and allow your heart to expand. Take a trip to the theater, play a favorite piece of music, see a film that moves you. You are able to connect with the arts because you see things in a bigger-than-life, theatrical way. Like the ancient Greeks, you know how to tell a story, and how to absorb one and allow it to change the beat of your heart. Take in any of the arts you love as a form of emotional nourishment. Bravo! Encore! Bravo!

Converse with Your Heart
Check in on your mood state a few times a day. Ask your heart to identify the mood you are in and how you can use your Moon sign's superpower—the power to inspire—to elevate your mood.

Virgo Moon: I am here to back you up when you say, "If you're going to do a job, do it right." Between you and me, I agree it is befuddling how half-assed so many people can be. We are different, though. We believe in honoring the activity at hand with our full attention and full commitment. That applies to everything from defrosting the refrigerator to proposing marriage. The little things count! And the big things, like lifelong love or saving the planet, can only happen when the tiny details are tended to.

Indeed, it can be hard on the heart when people make sarcastic remarks or belittle our good intentions and better deeds. But I am here to tell you that we are in the right. I know others may ask derisively, "Are you *always* right?" But the answer is a resounding *almost always*. Even if it is verboten to say that out loud!

Something that is good for our Virgoan soul is to go to

bed and remember all the good little deeds we did that day. They really add up. And since we don't mind making mistakes and learning from them, we can also "edit" our errors of the day in our mind. That way we'll get it one hundred percent right the next time. A+!

Converse with Your Heart
Check in on your mood state a few times a day. Ask your heart to identify the mood you are in and how you can use your Moon sign's superpower—the power to cultivate—to elevate your mood.

Libra Moon: Libra Moons like us need our sense of peace and equilibrium to be happy. Conflict makes us feel constricted and oppressed. No wonder we feel the need to retreat when fights begin. We would prefer to smooth over the difficult moments than allow sparks to turn into explosions.

Sometimes our best defense against people who can't stand peace and calm is to converse in a laid-back way. Maybe we shift the conversation from politics to pop music?

Even when we're alone but pensive with worry about work, love, money, or what have you, our nerves can become unsettled easily. A bit of luxury and mild laughter helps us a lot. Whether it's buying ourselves a pretty gift, luxuriating in the bath and our beautifications, or listening to a diverting podcast (and suddenly taking on the dialect of the calm Brits!), we need to create a bubble of calm to float in. Once we have our equilibrium back, we feel full of laughter and giddiness and may want to go to a party, take in a book reading, or create a great work of art.

Converse with Your Heart

Check in on your mood state a few times a day. Ask your heart to identify the mood you are in and how you can use your Moon sign's superpower—the power to harmonize—to elevate your mood.

Scorpio Moon: You are a riddle wrapped up in a mystery in a self-addressed stamped envelope marked ENIGMA, written in an obscure ancient alphabet. Sometimes we like it that way. When we are being challenged by people who don't see things our way, or even the ones who do but seem not to, we like to turn sphinxlike. Even though we are burning up with fire on the inside, we turn cold as ice on the outside to protect our hearts. Yes, that is what people don't understand about us when we are mad. First of all, when we are angry, anger may not be the primary emotion we are feeling. That is just how we react. We may actually be feeling misunderstood or even betrayed.

And let me tell you this: When people misunderstand you, I will always be here in your heart. I will "get" you. You won't need to explain your feelings or your behavior. Call upon me because I always have your back and understand your point of view.

One thing I can really help you with, though—hear me out on this one—is showing you how to slowly let down your guard and let the ones who really care in. It will be slow and cautious, like lowering oneself into a hot bath. But let's face it, you are deeply passionate, and although you *can* survive completely alone if you must, you would likely prefer the tenderness and laughter that comes with human connection.

And if you really just don't want to get past the truism "Hell is other people," then of course there is always the feline world there to serve as your companion.

Converse with Your Heart
Check in on your mood state a few times a day. Ask your heart to identify the mood you are in and how you can use your Moon sign's superpower—the power to transform—to elevate your mood.

Sagittarius Moon: Boy, can't anyone in this world take a joke anymore? You just try to lighten the mood and keep the conversation breezy, then shift the volume up to hilarity, and suddenly someone gets offended. I mean, isn't a quick joke in response to the ruffled feathers enough to bring everybody together again? You have a big, noble heart, so if you have really hurt someone, you know just how to take it on the chin and bring the goodwill back.

Just make sure to not self-censor. You understand that life is meant to be fun, that people are meant to crack up together, to explore fascinating obsessions, to have adventures. When the hell did everyone get so uptight, so serious? I know you feel triggered even if you act the clown. But *I* remember what it was like when you were a kid and you were dismissed or threatened when you lit up a room. When your content was fabulous but your timing was off, according to the grown-ups. Maybe they used to say there's a time and place for everything. But they insisted on an "inside voice" even when you were outside! I know! That's how I remember it too!

Well, you're grown up now, and you've got me right here with you, telling you it's okay. You can "yes" them now if that's what's needed in an awkward moment. But when will they ever understand that "awkward" is not in your vocabulary?

Converse with Your Heart

Check in on your mood state a few times a day. Ask your heart to identify the mood you are in and how you can use your Moon sign's superpower—the power to explore—to elevate your mood.

Capricorn Moon: They say that Capricorns were "born old" and get younger as they age. At least they say that about Capricorn Sun people. But we Cap Moons can have it harder sometimes. In youth we may feel depressed, dark, and gloomy. And does it really get better as we age? They say that we were born when the Moon was in its "detriment." That sounds pretty crappy, doesn't it? Just because the Moon is more at home in a gushy sign like Cancer (our opposite), does that mean our more serious view of the world isn't valid? Of course not! We are able to see the world with an innate sense of wisdom. This is an asset when it comes to making big decisions.

You see the world in realistic terms, even if some just don't seem to have the maturity to get real.

I can offer you a couple techniques that could ease some of the angst that comes with just being you, though. First, your sense of humor is bawdier than most people realize.

So get down and dirty and enjoy your earthiness, I say. Another thing that helps is to know that you're a boss. However bad the world gets, you have the power to think your way through it. Maybe you need to keep that to yourself when odds are against you, but know that I am there, seeing you for who you are. The main thing to keep in mind is that you need to talk to yourself in a real way. Give yourself praise for your emotional clarity, your innate maturity, and your way of using humor to turn a tough time around.

Converse with Your Heart

Check in on your mood state a few times a day. Ask your heart to identify the mood you are in and how you can use your Moon sign's superpower—the power to strategize—to elevate your mood.

Aquarius Moon: Sometimes it may sound nice to be programmed like a robot and to shift into a future where our innate human brilliance can be melded with technology and we can live in the beautiful world of intelligence with a capital *I*. Instead (for now!), we have to put up with normies—the regular folks of the human race, whose favorite way to start a sentence is with "I."

What *we* really love is to pull back, as if we're looking through the most advanced telescope at the full beauty of the cosmos. I mean, when there is so much intelligence out there, it can feel boring to us to sit around with a bunch of navel-gazers. They seem to think they are the center of the universe. We know we are just specks. But while we are here, we are wired to use our brains to full capacity.

And you know what can shut a brain down quicker than

a glass of water on a hard drive? EMOTIONS! Yes, I know I am here as your Moon buddy, the friend who comes to your *emotional* rescue, but we both know that sometimes it feels like the world would be much friendlier without those irrational feelings bouncing all over the place.

On the other hand, it's nice to have companionship and to be with lovers or friends or colleagues who share our passion for knowledge and our noble wish to advance the human race. We want to make the world a better place, after all. And when we find others who share our altruistic natures, we warm up like sunshine and let our emotions flow. Another beautiful heart-centered trait you possess is your sense of acceptance for all. You are the least judgmental person in the room, and this quality truly allows your loved ones to be themselves fully.

Converse with Your Heart

Check in on your mood state a few times a day. Ask your heart to identify the mood you are in and how you can use your Moon sign's superpower—the power to invent—to elevate your mood.

Pisces Moon: They say we are too sensitive. That we live in a fantasy world. So what if that's true? Fantasy is the sibling to imagination, and imagination is part and parcel of empathy. We have so much compassion for others, can't they extend a little understanding for us sometimes?

Yes, it's true we can be taken advantage of. But let's face it, we would rather give than receive. It makes us feel an expansion of our heart. And just between you and me, isn't it fun to be the one who takes the high road? That way we don't suffer from guilt or get bad press. We like to put others before us because that's the right thing to do, but it doesn't hurt to be put on a pedestal for our kindness sometimes, does it? (Insert evil laughter here.)

And when other people get to be too much, we always have music! We are naturally tuned in to timeless vibrations that take us to other worlds. Using our creativity does that for us too. It feels so good to invent stories and bring dreams to life, doesn't it?

Converse with Your Heart
Check in on your mood state a few times a day. Ask your heart to identify the mood you are in and how you can use your Moon sign's superpower—the power to imagine—to elevate your mood.

RISING SIGN (YOUR WORK-YOUR-BODY BUDDY)

Your Rising sign is the member of your friend group who helps you tune in to your body's messages. Call upon this member of your High-Vibe Tribe when you need some help understanding what your body needs and what your body is trying to tell you. In the section that follows, you will discover the part of the body ruled by your individual Rising sign and how best to tap into its messages for you. You may also be advised to align your chakras. Chakras are the energy centers in your body that hold prana, or life force. If the prana gets stuck in one particular area, you may feel energetically blocked. But you can align your chakras through meditation or a yoga practice. (Of course, if you're experiencing really severe pain anywhere, you should call your doctor or go to the ER.)

Aries Rising: We rule the head and Mars rules our sign—Mars being the planet of war. So it shouldn't surprise you to know that I totally get it when you feel like your head is going to explode! Sometimes our adrenaline kicks in so strongly that it feels like we're operating at warp speed. But listen, here's how I can help you, my dude.

If you are feeling explosive, try immediately putting your hands to your head. Give yourself a head and face massage. Don't think, just let your fingers do the walking. Imagine a red ball of fire in your head. With eyes closed, watch it speed quickly around your skull. Take a deep breath and feel it slow down just a notch as its color fades a tiny bit. Keep taking deep breaths as you repeat this exercise five times. If you need to go to ten, please do. If you need to keep going until the red becomes white and the ball is now moving at the speed of a sloth, wonderful!

Converse with Your Head

Ask your head what message it wants to communicate to you. If it replies in symbols or metaphor, take a minute to ask yourself what they mean. Send extra love and peace to your head. Ask it what the next step is you need to take.

Taurus Rising: We rule the neck and throat. When we are feeling constricted, like we want to say something but we don't feel safe, that's when our throat signals us. We Taurus

Rising folk might be worried that we have reached our boiling point and will get too rough with others. Or perhaps we are swallowing our real feelings out of fear of rocking the boat. No wonder! Venus is our planetary ruler, and she's a lover, not a fighter.

At times like these, our throat chakra is signaling that it must be opened to let our authentic voice come through. Sometimes just to recognize how we feel is enough. And sometimes shifting the mood with music—to soothe the savage beast—helps a lot.

Treating our throat with honey or hot water with lemon can be soothing too. And really, that's what we need most in tense situations: to feel comforted and cared for.

We've got to make sure we pay attention to our neck too. It can get stiff and strained when we have dug in too deep. When we are so sure we're right and too adverse to change, our neck may signal that we are being too immovable.

Converse with Your Neck and Throat

Ask your neck what it is worried about. And pay attention to the answer. Breathe in to the count of four, and exhale to the count of eight. Try it a few times and you will feel calmer and more lucid. And ask your throat, "What is it I need to say that I am swallowing down?"

Gemini Rising: Our sign rules the hands. Is it a wonder we talk with ours? If we start to get issues with our hands—sprained fingers, or if we cut ourselves or bite our nails raw—it usually is a message. Our superhero identity is the Messenger, after all. Often our hands are trying to communicate that we are anxious. Have you noticed that sometimes it's hard to ascertain the difference between excitement and anxiety?

When your nerves are jangly and you don't feel grounded, that's when you call upon me. That's the time that deep breathing is called for. We Geminis are air signs, and we are ruled by Mercury, the planet of nervous energy. Gemini is also in charge of the lungs. Some deep, deep breathing can help us calm our bodies and get out of our heads and into our hearts. That's where the real intel comes from.

Converse with Your Hands

Touch each fingertip to your thumb, one at a time, forming an O sign. Do this ten times on each hand, and your mind will stop racing. Also ask your hands, "What do you want to communicate to me?" Try closing your eyes and imagining your finger pointing. What is it pointing to? What do you think this image is telling you?

Cancer Rising: It's been established that we can be a sensitive sign. But I'm going to remind you how joyous we can be too—when we are in the setting we desire. When we want to be outside and are forced to stay inside, we could get surly or silent. Sometimes we have to adjust to environments that are not ideal for us, but even in those situations, we can use tools to elevate our mood. Maybe it's by just drinking water (we are ruled by water) or imagining ourselves at the beach or by a lake.

Cancer rules the chest, which signifies nurturing, but it is most important that we nurture ourselves, not just all the people who need us! The chest also signals to us when we are feeling heartbreak or emotional pain. Sending love to this area of our body is very important.

Converse with Your Chest
Ask it what you are really feeling. For example, if you feel a sense of emptiness, you could ask, "Why do I feel so disconnected from my feelings?" Your chest will help you align with your authentic emotional state and advise you on what you need to "feed" your soul.

Leo Rising: I am the member of your High-Vibe Tribe who helps you tune in to your body. Your gorgeous physical self holds more wisdom than you know! Our sign rules the heart and the upper back, both such strong areas of the body. And Leo the Leader, you are formidable! But conversely, when life hits you like a ton of bricks, you also fall hard.

Your back holds a lot of weariness. You often push through life so hard to get to the top, to meet your goals, to be the best person you can be—and there's only so much you can take! Take extra-good care of your back, whether that means regular massages, long baths, or luxurious stretching. Don't let self-care like this be an afterthought.

Your heart also needs some special lovin'. Some say you have the biggest heart of all, and with that comes the occasional heartbreak. You see love as an unlimited treasure, one which you want to share with the world, especially those you hold close. Most of the time this draws people to you. They want to know how they can be as openhearted as you. But on occasion, you give your love to someone who takes it for granted. And that really hurts! When you are feeling beaten down, it's very important to treat yourself the way you would a lover or best friend or child: with over-the-top generosity. Spoil yourself not just with material luxuries (which only work as a distraction) but with complete adoration. Remind yourself what makes you *you*.

Converse with Your Heart

Arrange a heart-to-heart talk in your mind, out loud, or on the page. Ask your heart, "What kind of love do we need from the people in our life?" or "What is the best way for us to emotionally take care of ourselves?" Breathe into your heart center, and tune in to your heart chakra. Open up to the messages of how you can love yourself better.

Virgo Rising: You may hear people say Virgos are worriers. And that worries us! And our worries sometimes act up in the area of the body our sign rules: the digestive system. If we get nervous, we first feel it in our bellies. I am your body buddy, baby, and I'm here to tell you that you are at your best when you take extra-good care with what you eat. If you notice certain foods trigger you, try cutting down on them. Your belly is just as serious as you are and won't stop nagging you until you listen.

But there is another kind of belly pain that may arise that has nothing to do with your culinary habits. Pain may occur when you have trouble "digesting" certain issues in your life. Perhaps there is something going on in a relationship that doesn't "sit well" with you. Or maybe old family angst or current issues with money are swirling around inside you, making mild aches turn into acute pain.

Your digestive system wants you to deal with whatever is really ailing you. Your habit is to work harder when challenges arise. But I am here to tell you that, in moments of turmoil that you feel in your belly, you need to stop and meditate on what is really going on. Whatever immediate work you are worried about can wait. *You* are more important than a project deadline. (However, if you're experiencing severe pain, you should call your doctor or go to the ER.)

Converse with Your Digestive System

Ask your gut where your blind spot is. It will tell you what you have been ignoring, which is likely the real culprit behind your belly problems. Perhaps ask a practical (very Virgoan!) question like, "What do we need right this moment?" Perhaps it's a chamomile tea or a phone call to a bestie. Put your hands on your belly and breathe into them, all the while listening to what your body needs to communicate.

Libra Rising: Ruled by Venus, planet of beauty, we Librans care about harmonious presentation. Our sign rules the lower back and buttocks. If you ever feel as if you have a sudden pain in your lower back, or you are feeling out of balance as you walk, please call upon me. I'm the member of your High-Vibe Tribe who can help you tune in to the nuanced messages your body is sending. We are a sign of subtlety, and it takes care and patience to figure out what our body is trying to tell us.

The buttocks/glutes help us a great deal with balance while we are walking and with maintaining stability. (And of course, having a cute ass is always a plus. Just being real here!) Making sure we build strength in that area is really important for us. And if you find your lower back starting to cave and your posture not up to snuff, it could be your body trying to get your attention.

Perhaps your self-esteem is getting a bit low. Are you angry at yourself? Ashamed? I am here to remind you to be proud of the kind, elevated creature you are. If you are having a bad spell, perhaps you need to get your ass in a chair and journal a bit to ascertain where this negative self-talk is being directed. And then act as a mediator, letting the negative talker know that you appreciate their opinion, but you prefer to take the kind-love approach, not tough love, with yourself.

Converse with Your Lower Back and Glutes: Is there an area of life where you are caving in, where you are not standing up for yourself, where you are off-balance? Talk to your lower back and glutes and ask them to clue you in to your blind spot. Since making decisions is not always easy for you, ask your body for guidance on what choice to make.

Scorpio Rising: We have a very sexy reputation, and in keeping with that, of course our sign rules the genitals and pelvis. But we are a sign of symbols and metaphor, so beyond the literal, I'm here to point out the higher messages your body is sending you. This area of the body is associated with the sacral chakra. It is connected to our reproductive system, and more than that to our sexuality and creativity. Interestingly, our spiritual urges and expression are linked to our creative urges and expression. If we are out of balance and spending too much time dwelling in our lower desires, we need to snap ourselves out of it.

Transmuting sexual energy into spiritual or creative energy will give you a boost of optimism and help you release some of the intensity you are holding on to. You are a person of great depth, but sometimes your energy gets stuck in one place. Making sure your chakras are balanced is especially important for you, love. That's how your charged electrical charisma operates most fully and also how you keep yourself emotionally stable.

Converse with Your Genitals and Pelvis

You know what it feels like to be all riled up, so tune in to this area of your body and ask for help finding peace. Your body is the vessel that holds your spirit and helps you maintain equilibrium. Your Higher Self will talk to you through your body when you remember to actively engage with it. It might give you messages about where you hold hurts and how to release them.

Sagittarius Rising: We Sag folks tend to use our bodies a lot. Athleticism often comes easy to us. But be careful with that flexible bod of yours! We're also known to be a little clumsy, so watch where you're going! Ruled by Jupiter, the planet of good luck and expansion, things usually turn out just great even when we make mistakes and bang up our bods a bit. One thing to remember about Jupiter, though, is that it can be a little excessive. The tendency to overeat or overdo the good life is a habit to keep in check. Go crazy having a good time. But not every day.

Our sign rules the hips and thighs. As we age, the hips get tighter and stretching becomes much more important. Remember to warm up before or after you play sports or exercise. And remember, too, although you've got a great set of gams, you also need to treat them well. Check in with your body before you use it and bruise it.

Converse with Your Hips and Thighs

If you are feeling uptight, your hips might have a few good messages for you. Ask yourself: What is making you feel like you can't be yourself? And if you feel a strain or a pulling in your thighs, perhaps it's best to tune in to your legs and reassess where you're running to and why—or what or whom you are running away from.

Capricorn Rising: Our sign rules the knees and joints, so it's important that we pay attention when we don't feel "loose" or our body starts making creaky sounds. Beyond just natural aging, it is sometimes a clue that we are feeling disjointed. Capricorns, ruled by disciplined Saturn, tend to work super hard, and we usually have a goal in mind. But sometimes the steps along the way could be a little disconnected. You need to feel like you are present when working, not just phoning in your hours and sweat.

Presence is best achieved when you tune in to your body. Remember, Capricorn is an earth sign. Earth signs are the most physical of the elements. If you are spending too much time strategizing in your head and not enough time tuning in to your body, you need to shift gears.

Keep in mind, too, that your knees are your friends! Knees symbolize humility—the way we get down on our knees to pray. In what area of your life do you need to show more humility? Perhaps you would simply benefit from a gratitude practice. Capricorns are known to have Saturnian (dark) natures. When we take time to acknowledge what we are grateful for, our moods naturally lighten.

Converse with Your Knees and Joints
Ask your knees if you are "bowing down" to outside forces too much. If yes, ask for guidance on how to shift your behavior to take better care of yourself. Ask if you perhaps need to bow down more—as in giving more thanks for what you have rather than focusing on what you lack.

Aquarius Rising: Aquarius, we are known to be brilliant and inventive. Our superhero identity is that of the Visionary. But life does not begin and end with the mind. Our sign rules the calves and ankles, and it is amazing how much we rely on them. Instead of walking down the street, having a brilliant conversation with earbuds in, how about stepping mindfully along our path? This isn't just good for our body, it's good for whatever we are trying to accomplish too.

Ankles can be prone to twisting. An injury or even a close call might be the body's way of alerting you to your unconscious state of mind. Are you feeling pulled in many directions? Are you being inflexible in your decision-making?

Sometimes it's necessary to stop and reassess *why* we are doing what we are doing.

As for the calves, the left calf is associated with the inner world and the right calf with the outer. Depending on where you have an injury or an issue, you may want to dedicate more time to understanding your choices and motivations in either area of your life.

Converse with Your Calves and Ankles

The ankles may be prone to slipping. Ask your ankles—either aloud, in your imagination, or on paper—where you might be slipping. Where are you setting yourself up for a fall? The calves lend themselves to stability and quietly keep you moving well. Talk to them about where you might be out of balance in your life or in your thinking.

Pisces Rising: Our sign is ruled by Neptune, the planet of dreams and illusion. Although Neptune gifts us great imagination, it can sometimes leave us feeling confused in the outer world. Pisces rules the feet—an area of the body that has much to say spiritually. Ask yourself: Are you standing on your own two feet? What would make you feel more grounded? The feet point us in a direction. Are you happy with the direction you are going in, or is it time to reassess?

Feet can be associated with the root chakra in different cultures. This signifies our sense of security in the world. Do you feel unsafe? What would make you feel more secure?

If you are feeling out of sorts or confused, or if you've suffered a foot injury, sit down and talk to me! I'm the member of your High-Vibe Tribe that can serve as translator between body and spirit.

Let's start with what you are most afraid about right now. Tell me all about it. I'm here to listen and to guide.

Converse with Your Feet

When you've injured your feet, or even if they're just feeling a little weary, it's time to slow down, put them up, and have a heart-to-heart conversation. Or heart-to-foot. Or . . . you know what I mean! Ask your feet what guidance they can give you. Ask them if you need to end a chapter in your life and start a new one. And if so, where to begin? You could also ask for specific techniques to help you stay grounded in this turbulent world.

STEP FOUR

Manifesting Your Dream Life

THIS SECTION IS WHERE WE PUT ALL THE STEPS TOGETHER. It contains exercises, meditations, and mantras to practice with clear intention and an open heart.

To recap: You have learned three key pieces of wisdom:

- What to expect from the 20-year Pluto in Aquarius era
- What your new zodiac avatar's superpowers are and how to use them
- How to collaborate with your Big-Three High-Vibe Tribe for wisdom and guidance

So, before we pull out the alchemy cauldron and start a-stirring, let's talk a little bit about how I see manifestation. To bring a desire to life in the third-dimensional (embodied) world, you must first become the version of yourself who already has what you want. If you have ever been a child, you already know how to do this! Most people have lost their childlike ability to suspend disbelief by the time they reach adulthood. But it doesn't have to be that way. Nor do you have to go full-on delusional and convince yourself you are a different person.

All you have to do is tune in to what you imagine you'd *feel* when you receive your desire. Do you desire respect for your talents? What does that feel like in your body, especially in your heart center? Let's say a feeling of pride and joy rises up in your chest. Perhaps you see yourself at a podium receiving an award. Hold on to that feeling and imagine the version of you that would be there on stage. It's certainly not an insecure, self-defeating version of you, right? You want to get to know this happy, accomplished person. So in your everyday life, start to ask yourself: How would *that* person make their coffee, walk down the street, and spend their free time?

It is very actorly! To benefit from this approach, you need to suspend disbelief.

Once you get the swing of it, you will become the super-powered version of yourself who you connected with in Step Two. And don't forget your High-Vibe Tribe from Step Three who will be there to help guide you through the smaller steps.

Here in Step Four you will find a series of exercises, meditations, and mantras to help you on your path. Play with them and have fun!

ACCESSING A TRANCELIKE STATE

Before you dive in, here is a simple tip for slowing down your brain waves and accessing a mild trancelike state:

Get into a comfortable position. Allow your body to sink into your seat or bed or floor. Breathe deeply and just focus on the feeling of your inhalation and your exhalation. When your mind wanders, it's okay, just come back to the breath and continue. Do this for a few minutes until you feel like you've gone inward. Accessing this state will help you when you are doing the bulk of these exercises.

EXERCISE NUMBER ONE

The Mandala

Draw a mandala based on your astrological superhero. Traditionally, a mandala is based on geometric shapes found in nature and the cosmos. But your mandala can be anything. Here are the steps to follow:

1. Ideally, use a large piece of drawing paper. Draw a big circle. Find different-colored markers or crayons to work with. Meditation or classical music or tunes without words are recommended. Set a timer for 15 minutes. Draw whatever comes to you based on your connection to your superhero self and your superpowers.

2. When the timer goes off, give yourself more time if you need it.

3. Put your name and date on the drawing.

4. Once you're finished, pin your drawing up or lay it in any way that allows you to stare at it for a few minutes, as you would a painting in a gallery.

5. What do you see? Make notes in your journal. Keep the mandala handy so that during the week you can use it as the focus of meditation and to "trance-out" while seeking answers to relevant questions.

EXERCISE NUMBER TWO

Automatic Writing with Your High-Vibe Tribe

Automatic writing is writing that we do in a somewhat trancelike state. Your High-Vibe Tribe is here to help you with this one!

Set a timer for 10 minutes or fill one page. You can certainly write more, but try this at minimum. In your journal, write a dialogue between you, your Sun, your Moon, and your Rising signs. Let your Tribe know what you'd like some guidance on.

Remember that your Sun is in charge of your mind, your Moon is in charge of your heart, and your Rising is in charge of your body. Keep in mind that automatic writing is all about letting the words flow and not censoring yourself. So even if what you write doesn't make sense on first read, it's okay. Just keep going.

The best way to approach this exercise is to begin with what is on your mind and ask your Tribe for guidance. Allow a dialogue to emerge, and at the end ask the Tribe for their final recommendation. Here is a sample mini-version:

Me: I am worried about my friends pulling away from me. What should I do?

ARIES SUN: That is rough. Describe the situation.

Me: I used to get together with our gang once a month, and now it's been over six months . . .

LIBRA MOON: How are you feeling right at this moment?

Me: Abandoned and a little scared.

TAURUS RISING: Where do you feel it in your body?

Dialogue continues, and then at the end . . .

ARIES SUN: Let the three of us come together to help you. Moon, Rising, what should we advise?

HIGH-VIBE TRIBE: Before you take any steps, ask yourself: What are you feeling scared about? Allow yourself to feel those rough feelings, and then try to give yourself what you think your friends would give you if you were out together right now. They would likely remind you how strong you really are and that you always find your way through life's challenges.

Ask yourself what the takeaway of this exercise was. What was the message? Don't overthink. Just answer this question right away and write it down. Make sure to thank your High-Vibe Tribe. They are always there for you and really appreciate your gratitude!

EXERCISE NUMBER THREE

Alchemize and Internalize Your Big Three

Draw a picture of each of your Big-Three High-Vibe Tribe members. The drawings don't need to be advanced. They can be as simple or complex as you wish. Use colored markers or crayons. When you're done, start a new drawing that takes elements of each of the three characters and blends them together so they form one new face. Imagine this face as the love child of your Big-Three High-Vibe Tribe!

Allow yourself a minute or two to breathe and slow down your brain waves as you stare at this final drawing. Imagine this is a new friend in your life who possesses tremendous wisdom, kindness, and humor.

Invite this new friend to live inside of you, like an invisible spiritual buddy. Practice over the next day or so saying hi to your buddy. Converse in your mind with them. Over time you will find yourself making decisions and choices with the input of this very special pal!

✵ EXERCISE NUMBER FOUR ✵

Engage with Your Kryptonite (Movement Exercise)

All superheroes have their kryptonite. The term refers to Superman's particular reaction to a mineral from an alien planet that deprives him of his superpowers.

What is yours? You may get some insight by rereading the "Supershadow" section of your sign's chapter. But to get a more specific sense of your individual kryptonite, try this exercise. Feel free to make an audio recording of these steps to help you with the process.

1. Choose an area where you feel comfortable and where you have space and privacy.

2. Stand in an X position, legs wide and arms spread above you, reaching for the sky.

3. Swivel your body clockwise, keeping your arms outstretched.

4. Swivel your body counterclockwise.

5. Imagine you possess the power of flight and are flying through the air, feeling strong and joyful. Breathe in and out slowly and deeply to help elevate your mood.

6. Tune in to your superhero name and your superpower. When you connect to them, where does your imagination go?

7. Enjoy this process for a minute or two.

8. Impulsively duck for cover. Imagine a person, creature, or substance suddenly drains you of your powers.

9. Curl into a fetal position and play dead for a minute or two so that you can get your bearings.

10. Without knowing what will come out of your mouth, start addressing your kryptonite. Give it a name, even if it's a nonsense word. But try to tap into what or whom it reminds you of. A type of person? A situation? Something you fear?

11. Talk to it quietly and ask it why it is playing this role in your life and how you can coexist together in the same world.

You have just suspended disbelief in this game of pretend. Afterward, take note of how this particular kryptonite affects you in your day-to-day life—and how you can creatively maintain your powers or work around its effects.

EXERCISE NUMBER FIVE

The Magic Window of Consciousness

What is the first thing you think of when you hear the word *hypnagogia*?

"WTF is that?"

"Is it contagious?"

No need to panic! It simply refers to an absolutely lovely state of consciousness—that magical window between being awake and falling asleep, and between being asleep and waking up. (Technically, the latter is called hypnopompia, but that word always reminds me of a pompous hippo, so let's stick with hypnagogia, which can be used to cover both.)

Appreciating and tapping into how your mind is working in a hypnagogic state can help you as you're manifesting your best life. This exercise is meant to connect you to your unconscious self, your intuitive self. This is the part of you that *knows* the guidance you need, whereas your conscious mind stays at a surface level. Here are some presleep and postsleep practices you can try that may help you benefit from this special state of consciousness:

- Before sleep, get into the habit of keeping a notebook or other note-taking device by your bed. When you feel drowsy, like you might be falling asleep soon, set an intention. What you're going to do here is collab with your superhero alter ego to help you attain an answer or some guidance on a quandary. You could ask, "What would help me feel better about my body?" or "What path should I take with this creative project?" Put it out there, then let it go and allow yourself to drift off to sleep.
- When you wake up in the morning (or in the middle of the night), write down what your superhero alter ego tells you. Think of this as instructions you are getting from your boss. And you have a great boss! Don't worry if it takes some time to build up this practice. Over time you will train yourself to ask for what you need, and to receive and write down the answers.
- In the morning, also try this: Before you get lost scrolling on your phone or dealing with the outside world, try having a conversation on the page with your superhero alter ego. Keep it stream of

consciousness. A few pages or ten minutes is good. Doing this while you're still in that magic window between sleeping and waking will give you a lot of bang for your buck!

✵ EXERCISE NUMBER SIX ✵

Glyph of the Day

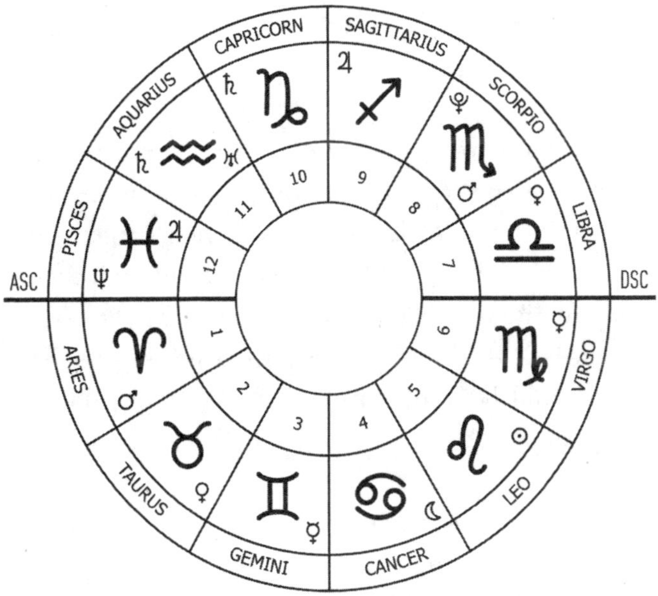

Each zodiac sign has its own glyph—a symbolic representation that dates back to the ancient Babylonian and Greek civilizations. They are a shorthand astrologers use when constructing charts. When we speak, we cast a *spell* of sorts (why do you think it's called *spelling*?), and in a similar way we can tune in to the visual symbols to access the quantum field of possibilities.

To practice connecting with these visual symbols, I recommend the following exercise:

1. Get into a comfortable position and stare at the chart of the twelve glyphs. Allow your eyes to glaze over. Take a few minutes to look at each individual symbol. Then look at them as a group again. When you're ready, close your eyes and see which glyph pops into your head first.

2. You can either open your eyes and draw the glyph to stare at for another minute or two or just stare at it on the page with the others again, but focus now on just the one glyph you saw in your mind.

3. Now close your eyes again for a few minutes and ask the glyph to guide you to the quantum field of possibilities. This is the energetic field we exist in during each individual moment, and within it there are infinite possible realities we can align with. You could ask the glyph, "What am I not seeing that you could help me with?" and "What should my next steps be?"

4. For instance, something as small as going to get your coffee on the west side of town instead of the east could lead you to unexpected occurrences, like running into someone you really need to talk to or avoiding a traffic jam. A bigger example could be talking to your partner about a relationship problem versus sitting with it yourself for 24 hours. Let the glyph be your guide!

5. When you are done, make a note of what came up and what your takeaway from the exercise was.

6. Note which sign the glyph is associated with, peruse a little about that sign in Step Two (pages 17–167), then let the glyph hang out in the back of your mind the rest of the day. Make sure to say thanks!

EXERCISE NUMBER SEVEN

Analyze a Friend's Big Three

This is something fun to do for a friend or with a friend.

Obtain the Sun, Moon, and Rising signs for your buddy. Divide a blank page into three sections. Write the following notes down, filling in the blanks: "___ Sun," in another "___ Moon," and in the third, "___ Rising."

Based on your instincts and what you read about each sign in Step Two, make notes about the qualities of each sign that connect to your friend. Keep in mind, some will not be obvious. Dig deep and allow your intuition to come through.

See what each of the Big Three symbolizes. The Sun is associated with the mind, the Moon with the heart, and the Rising with the body. Free-associate how these qualities play out for your friend. For example, if your BFF has a Moon in Sagittarius, she may love to make jokes to lighten her own mood.

When you are done, look at the three signs—your friend's High-Vibe Tribe—and come up with a few sentences that capture the essence of her character. Then see if you can cull them into a spiritual message. In other words, why might she be incarnated now? What is her soul's mission? Discuss with her.

EXERCISE NUMBER EIGHT

Astrological Tarot Reading

Here is a guide to the astrological correspondences of the tarot cards.

Major Arcana

- **Aries:** The Emperor
- **Taurus:** The Hierophant, The Empress
- **Gemini:** The Lovers, The Magician
- **Cancer:** The Chariot, The High Priestess, The Moon
- **Leo:** The Sun, Strength
- **Virgo:** The Hermit
- **Libra:** Justice
- **Scorpio:** Death
- **Sagittarius:** Temperance, Judgment
- **Capricorn:** The Devil
- **Aquarius:** The Star, The Hanged Man
- **Pisces:** The Moon
- **All Signs:** The Fool
- **All Fixed Signs (Taurus, Leo, Scorpio, Aquarius):** The Wheel of Fortune

Aces and Court Cards: Pages, Knights, Queens, and Kings

- **Wands (fire):** Aries, Leo, and Sagittarius
- **Pentacles (earth):** Taurus, Virgo, and Capricorn
- **Swords (air):** Gemini, Libra, and Aquarius
- **Cups (water):** Cancer, Scorpio, and Pisces

Numbered Cards

- The twos, threes, and fours correspond to the cardinal signs.
- The fives, sixes, and sevens correspond to the fixed signs.
- The eights, nines, and tens correspond to the mutable signs.
- Below they are broken down by suit and element.

Wands (Fire):

- Two, Three, Four: **ARIES**
- Five, Six, Seven: **LEO**
- Eight, Nine, Ten: **SAGITTARIUS**

Pentacles (Earth):

- Two, Three, Four: **CAPRICORN**
- Five, Six, Seven: **TAURUS**
- Eight, Nine, Ten: **VIRGO**

Swords (Air):

- Two, Three, Four: **LIBRA**
- Five, Six, Seven: **AQUARIUS**
- Eight, Nine, Ten: **GEMINI**

Cups (Water):

- Two, Three, Four: **CANCER**
- Five, Six, Seven: **SCORPIO**
- Eight, Nine, Ten: **PISCES**

To Perform a Card Reading for Yourself (Or a Friend)

1. Shuffle the cards. Mix them up any way you want to. Close your eyes and ask the universe, the spirit world, God, whatever works for you—for some guidance. Some people use this time to set an intention.

2. Pull three cards and place them face down.
   - Left is for the past.
   - Middle is for the present.
   - Right is for the future.

3. Flip them over to read. I always read cards face up, not upside down, but you may do as you wish. Note: Major arcana cards often suggest that what you are asking about is of greater importance. Aces suggest new beginnings. Major arcana cards or aces also suggest a "yes" answer if that's what you are inquiring about. Try to tap into your intuition before looking up the meaning of a card. Use the astrological correspondences to make connections.

4. Decide what you want to ask about on a more focused level, but keep your question open-ended, not yes or no. Relationships, career, and money tend to be the subjects people most often inquire about.

5. If you have further questions, pull more cards. Sometimes one card will answer a specific question, sometimes three.

6. Reshuffle and pull a final meditation card. Ask the universe for something to keep in mind, a final thought for the time being.

7. If you want to do a reading about a relationship, I suggest splitting the deck into three sections after shuffling. Put the one you intuit represents the other person on the right. Put the pile for yourself to the left. Place the pile for the relationship in the middle. Turn over the top cards for each (they represent the external parts), then pull out the bottom cards for each (they represent the hidden parts) and intuit the meaning. Use the astrological correspondences to make connections.

EXERCISE NUMBER NINE

I Ching Reading

The Chinese I Ching or Book of Changes is an ancient oracle system dating back over 5,000 years, based on the concepts of yin the feminine and yang the masculine. Those who wish to divine the future or bask in contemplation have long turned to the I Ching for guidance. It's made up of sixty-four hexagrams, each of which presents a situation to meditate on and "rehearse" how you could deal with a similar scene in earthly life. Practicing the I Ching allows you to develop your intuition and self-knowledge, just as studying astrology can. The hexagrams consist of broken and unbroken lines that represent the masculine and feminine aspects of nature, respectively. In astrology, the fire and air signs represent archetypal masculine energy, and the earth and water signs represent archetypal feminine energy.

The oracle of the I Ching has lived in conversation with spiritual seekers for over three thousand years. In ancient times, yarrow sticks were used. Later, coins took their place (thus the "toss the I Ching" expression) before tarot-style cards (my preference) and now apps. There will no doubt be more advanced technological ways to consult the I Ching. But what is so great about this form of divination is that you may also go completely analog. If you are on a camping trip or living in end-times (!), you can simply gather up sticks and create hexagrams from them. Or draw the hexagrams on scraps of paper, throw them in a hat, choose one of the 64, and see what message it gives you. If you want to be a good Cub Scout, you could prepare a set ahead of time as a craft project. Then you can take them with you anywhere!

So what is a hexagram? A hexagram consists of six lines, forming any combination of yin and yang lines. The yin (feminine) lines are broken and the yang (masculine) are unbroken. Each of the sixty-four hexagrams contains a unique combination of lines. The placement of each line has a special meaning, and the lines are counted from the bottom up:

- Line #6: Reflection
- Line #5: Taking charge
- Line #4: Planning
- Line #3: Transition
- Line #2: Feelings
- Line #1: Beginnings

Ask a question and see what hexagram comes up to answer you. Each of the sixty-four hexagrams has its own special meaning. To study the I Ching in depth, I recommend the translation of the Book of Changes by Richard Wilhelm. What follows is a quick shorthand for the hexagrams' meanings.

When doing this exercise, tune in to your superhero alter ego for more insight into its meaning on a practical level.

䷀	Hexagram 1:	Yang. Creative movement. A brand-new start, beginnings.
䷁	Hexagram 2:	Yin. Receptivity, openness.
䷂	Hexagram 3:	Beginnings can be challenging; it is a normal part of new endeavors.
䷃	Hexagram 4:	Youthful naivete.
䷄	Hexagram 5:	Be ready when opportunity strikes. Patience is a virtue.
䷅	Hexagram 6:	Conflict. Mediation may be called for to resolve disagreements.
䷆	Hexagram 7:	The Army, symbolizing collective strength, organization, and structure.
䷇	Hexagram 8:	The ties that bind. Sticking together.
䷈	Hexagram 9:	Small actions are significant now. Take baby steps and hang in there.
䷉	Hexagram 10:	Mindful, careful action.

䷊	Hexagram 11:	Peace and harmony. The union of opposing forces.
䷋	Hexagram 12:	Standstill and stagnation. Meditate on the meaning of obstacles.
䷌	Hexagram 13:	Companionship. Shared goals for the future.
䷍	Hexagram 14:	Abundance and prosperity.
䷎	Hexagram 15:	The importance of being humble and demure.
䷏	Hexagram 16:	Enthusiasm, highlighting passion, motivation, and the drive to achieve.
䷐	Hexagram 17:	Follow the flow of life.
䷑	Hexagram 18:	Address what has decayed. Restore what is broken. Renewal.
䷒	Hexagram 19:	Approach. After a period of retreat, closeness can begin again.
䷓	Hexagram 20:	Contemplation, stressing observation, introspection, and gaining perspective.
䷔	Hexagram 21:	Biting through. Face challenges and assure justice and clarity.

䷕ **Hexagram 22:** True beauty that emanates from the inside. Grace.

䷖ **Hexagram 23:** Splitting apart. Realizing what has become outmoded.

䷗ **Hexagram 24:** Returning to the light. A difficult cycle ends.

䷘ **Hexagram 25:** Innocence, good intentions. Being spontaneous.

䷙ **Hexagram 26:** A time of incubation leading to a return of greatness.

䷚ **Hexagram 27:** Nourishment. Self-care.

䷛ **Hexagram 28:** Balance may be called for. Calm the excess.

䷜ **Hexagram 29:** The Abysmal. Meditate on challenges, assess danger, and find the strength to keep going.

䷝ **Hexagram 30:** One who sees the light and brings clarity to others.

䷞ **Hexagram 31:** Influence, signifying attraction, connection, and the forces that draw entities together.

䷟ **Hexagram 32:** Endurance. Duration. Remain solid and expect renewal in good time.

䷠ Hexagram 33: Strategic withdrawal. Retreat. Turning inward.

䷡ Hexagram 34: The Power of the Great. Strength and vitality.

䷢ Hexagram 35: Advancement and progress. Positive momentum.

䷣ Hexagram 36: Times of trouble. Maintain your integrity and inner light. It will pass.

䷤ Hexagram 37: The Family. Domestic harmony.

䷥ Hexagram 38: Contrasts and opposing forces. Bring the parts that harmonize together and discard the rest.

䷦ Hexagram 39: Limping forward. Find another path and face fewer hurdles.

䷧ Hexagram 40: Deliverance. Liberty at last. Succeeding after a challenging time.

䷨ Hexagram 41: Decreasing. Keep anger and desire under control. Make a sacrifice in the short term for the sake of the long term.

䷩ Hexagram 42: Increasing growth. Period of expansion.

䷪ Hexagram 43: Breakthrough. Decision. A show of generosity and integrity.

䷫ Hexagram 44: Attraction. A new encounter. The feminine. Proceed with eyes open.

䷬ Hexagram 45: Gathering together. The power of collective action.

䷭ Hexagram 46: Pushing upward. A plant begins to grow.

䷮ Hexagram 47: Oppression, confinement. A need for a break or for comfort and relief.

䷯ Hexagram 48: The Well that nourishes. The eternal wisdom of the universe.

䷰ Hexagram 49: Revolution and radical change in the name of progress.

䷱ Hexagram 50: The Cauldron. A vessel for transmutation. Your purpose in life crystallizes.

䷲ Hexagram 51: Shock. Major disruptions in the outside world shake an individual to her core. But she can gather her wits to respond in a helpful, noble fashion.

䷳ Hexagram 52: Stillness. Introspection. Sometimes less is more.

䷴ Hexagram 53: Gradual progress. Nature knows what to do.

䷵ Hexagram 54: The path to union comes when we pay attention to the subtle nuances of a relationship.

䷶ Hexagram 55: The harvest. Fullness. Decisive action. Humility leads to good fortune.

䷷ Hexagram 56: Traveling. Wandering in search of knowledge.

䷸ Hexagram 57: Exerting influence in a quiet way.

䷹ Hexagram 58: Opening. Forces join together. A joyous time.

䷺ Hexagram 59: Dispersion. Chaos is followed by clarity.

䷻ Hexagram 60: Adhering to boundaries. Figuring out proper limits.

䷼ Hexagram 61: Inner truth. Maintain your authenticity while remaining open to new perspectives.

䷽ Hexagram 62: Small exceeding. Do more than what is asked of you and mind the details.

䷾ Hexagram 63: After Completion, reflecting on culmination of events and transitions occurring now or in the near future.

䷿ Hexagram 64: Before Completion. Make preparations and use good timing.

✵ EXERCISE NUMBER TEN ✵

Superhero Creative Movement

Put on music (preferably without words) and stand up tall. Close your eyes and breathe in the powers of your superhero alter ego. When you feel like you have embodied the spirit of your astrological superhero, begin to move around. After a few minutes, come up with three key movements you can put together as a piece of mini-choreography. You can do more if you like. You can also keep it super simple, like making a circle with you left pinky, sliding to the right, and shaking like a wet dog. Follow your instincts and have fun. You could also aim to use the body part that your Rising sign rules.

Once you've found the movements, set a timer for one minute and repeat them. Practice them as often as you like, knowing that is a way to activate your superhero identity.

✵ EXERCISE NUMBER ELEVEN ✵

Superhero Happy Dance

I think you know what this one is all about!

Use this exercise to celebrate when you're feeling great. Or use it when you're feeling down to improve your mood.

Put on some fun music and feel it vibrate through your body. Keep your eyes closed and shake out your limbs. Imagine that you are in full regalia, costumed as your superhero alter ego. Visualize yourself standing center stage in an animated film, when you suddenly break out into dance. Or, to put it in layman's terms: Bust a move! Do what comes naturally.

As you are winding down, imagine you are being called to come save the day. Ask yourself: Who needs my help? When you are done, make note of whom (a person in your life, a community organization, etc.) you felt called to help. Now, in real life, focus on offering some assistance.

You will find that giving of yourself and being of help to others makes you feel better about yourself and is a natural mood lifter.

EXERCISE NUMBER TWELVE

Superhero's Journey

The Hero's Journey is a narrative concept based on Joseph Campbell's studies of "monomyths," myths that exist across myriad cultures and time periods. This structure is now used regularly in storytelling. We see it on the screen and read it in books, and it resonates so much with viewers and readers thanks to the deeper truths of human experience it connects us to.

This exercise is meant to help you follow a yellow brick road of sorts to discover your best path to take to face a challenge, including the many steps to get you there. You know your superhero's name (from Aries the Warrior to Pisces the Dreamer). And you also know their greatest superpower. Here is a template to help you deal with situational challenges using your heroic gifts. Set a timer for fifteen minutes and see how far you get. If you need to reset the timer, do so as many times as you wish.

The steps below are adapted from the classic Hero's Journey narrative model. Apply them to your own life using the real and the imagined. When you're done, commit this story to memory like you would the plot of a novel or film. Committing your origin story to memory will eventually make it feel like part of your actual lived experience. The curious thing about the unconscious mind is this: It doesn't know the difference between what's real and what's imagined. Scientists have done studies on subjects who have "practiced" playing piano in their minds and found that the effects are equal to that of those who physically practice a composition. The term used is *mental practice*. The same holds true for expert athletes who practice their movements mentally and achieve greater success on the field. All of this is documented by the National Library of Medicine.

1. **The Ordinary World:** We meet our hero. *Write down what a typical day in your life is like right now.*

2. **Call to Adventure:** Will they meet the challenge? *What has just occurred that could spark your transformation from an average Joe to a superhero?*

3. **Refusal of the Call:** The hero resists the adventure. *What are you afraid of? What happens in your ordinary life now that something extraordinary has happened, but you haven't risen up to take the challenge?*

4. **Meeting the Mentor:** A teacher arrives. *Who could you ask for guidance just when you can't think clearly and don't know what to do? What do they say?*

5. **Crossing the First Threshold:** The hero leaves their comfort zone. *How do you leave everything that gives you a sense of routine and security? What steps do you take to officially cross over?*

6. **Tests, Allies, Enemies:** Making friends and facing roadblocks. *Here's where your High-Vibe Tribe will join you. Give each of the three a nickname and imagine what their special gift is. What enemies does your crew face? What makes them so powerful?*

7. **Approach to the Inmost Cave:** Getting closer to your goal. *Get down on your knees and pray to whatever you believe in. It could be your superhero self, or God, or the universe. Whatever works for you. You are close to reaching your goal, but you feel backed into a corner. What is going on and what are you praying for?*

8. **Ordeal:** The hero's biggest test yet! *What is the greatest challenge you've faced so far? What makes it so daunting? How do you feel, knowing the rough road that lies ahead?*

9. **Reward (Seizing the Sword):** Light at the end of the tunnel. *What wakes you up to the realization that you are now on a fantastic path? What is the potential reward for all you've endured?*

10. **The Road Back:** We aren't safe yet. *What dangers still await as you journey back home to your regular life?*

11. **Resurrection:** The final hurdle is reached. *You've met the challenge. You have won. How do you feel? How have you transformed?*

12. **Return with the Elixir:** The hero heads home, triumphant. *What will your life be like now that you have gone through your hero's journey?*

EXERCISE NUMBER THIRTEEN

Superhero Tool Belt

Every good superhero has a tool belt of some sort. This is where they keep the devices they may suddenly need. Spider-Man has a utility belt that holds web cartridges to refill his web shooters with. And later in Superman's history, he took a page from Batman's belt and started to wear one. In it, he keeps a secret supply of gold kryptonite to offset the destructive forces of his one weakness: kryptonite itself.

So what is on your tool belt?

- Write down your superhero's name and superpowers.
- Brainstorm what kind of tools they would carry on their person. Perhaps they carry a fidget toy or worry stone to help with anxiety. Maybe they carry a symbol of what they stand for—a heart, a plant?
- If you want, come up with kooky or creative names for them so they are easy to remember.

✵ EXERCISE NUMBER FOURTEEN ✵

Create Your Secret Superhero Cave

Batman has his Batcave, Superman his Fortress of Solitude. Where is your place to tune in to your superself?

In real life, transform a space in your home to act as a symbolic supercave. For example, in my home, I realized that I never used the meditation space I'd set up in my bedroom when I'd bought the house five years prior. And I meditate a lot! So I donated or tossed what I had never used. I found a lovely corner to put a small altar in. The idea of an antique mirror kept going through my head, so I bought one on eBay. One special cushion and a few doodads and tchotchkes later, and I was all set. Your supercave doesn't have to be big, just full of clear intention and good energy.

✵ EXERCISE NUMBER FIFTEEN ✵

Draw Your Ideal World

Take a big piece of construction paper, some colored pencils or markers (or use a device if you prefer), and draw a rectangular border. Now, within the lines, create the world you want to live in. It doesn't matter how well or poorly you think you draw. This is for you and is meant to be fun and eye-opening. It will help you see your vision of your ideal world come to life. Interesting and unexpected details you didn't even know you wanted may come up.

Here are the elements to include in your drawing:

- Home
- Loved ones

- Career
- Money
- Fun
- Community
- Surprises

Bring these areas to life by drawing them spontaneously. Allow inspiration to come by putting on music that puts you "in the mood" to envision your best life. Remember, the sky's the limit! You have superpowers.

✵ EXERCISE NUMBER SIXTEEN ✵

Your Definite Chief Aim (DCA)

I first came upon this term after reading *Think and Grow Rich*, a 1937 book by Napolean Hill. New Thought was a precursor to New Age, and it had a very whimsical, human spirit to it. The idea of New Thought was to change one's thinking to change one's life. This occurs by developing mental discipline, combined with techniques to access Divine (or Universal) Intelligence.

The idea of the DCA is simple. You identify your number one goal, the big one that you want to accomplish. Most often this refers to something worldly or work related. But it certainly could refer to other matters, like finding a romantic partner or having a baby. Once you know your DCA, your thinking shifts to organically take every step in service to this goal.

Most people are conditioned to listen to messages from the outside world, their family, friends, the culture at large. However, the only way to know what you *really* want is tune in to the *authentic* you, not the *conditioned-to-fit-in* you.

To get a sense of your DCA, try the following steps.

Meditate

Set a timer for five minutes and meditate to clear your mind. You can do it sitting up with back straight, lying down (my fave!), or whatever suits you. Focus on your breath. If your mind wanders (which it will), just come back to your inhalation, your exhalation. It doesn't matter how often you get distracted. Just keep coming back to your breath.

Journal with Your Higher Self

Next, set a timer for eight minutes. Write in your journal with the intention of uncovering your DCA. The key is to be completely uncensored. No one has to see this but you. Use a playscript format; that way you can have a dialogue with your Higher Self. I like to use my initials to represent my lines, and HS to represent the Higher Self speaking back to me, like so:

JD: *Please help me identify my DCA.*
HS: *What's the first thing that pops into your head?*
JD: *That I can't think of anything!*
HS: *If you could wave a magic wand and live your dream life, what would that look like and feel like?*

Decision Time

When that timer goes off, write down your DCA. If you need more time or if you can't narrow it down beyond three choices (Libra!), try again. But after two tries you have to come up with a working DCA. Remember, you don't have to know the *how* at this stage, just the *what*.

Wording of Your DCA

Here are some examples of the simplest way to write your DCA:

- I will publish a novel that touches people's lives worldwide.
- I will become a parent and raise a happy family with my beloved.
- I will work for myself and triple my income.

Read on if you want to try something more multifaceted.

Analog: Put your DCA on an index card, laminate it, and carry it around. Or keep it by your bedside so it's the first thing you see upon waking and the last thing you see before sleep.

Reverse Engineer: Imagine the end and use bullet points to work backward to ascertain what steps to take. Try six bullet points total. Number six is the end goal, number five the one that precedes it, and then all the way back to number one, a step you can take now.

Some advice about what steps you should take first: Do the "boring" tasks right away—whether that's filing paperwork, cleaning out a space, or reading technical manuals. Once you develop the habit of doing what's hard, it turns out it's not so hard after all.

Come Up with a Target Image: Imagine a scene that takes place when your wish is fulfilled, when you have accomplished your DCA. For instance, a dear supportive friend congratulates you, and your heart feels full. You are looking out through your eyes. If you want to live somewhere else, imagine what it feels like to wake up there, see the bed you have slept in, and get up and look out the window. You get the idea. The most important thing is to tap into the wonderful *feeling* you have when your desire is fulfilled. Write down the details of that image.

One Universal Note about Your DCA

Once you have identified it, keep it alive in your thoughts, words, and actions. That means that pretty much every decision you make, small and large, revolves around bringing your DCA to life. You should still be having fun—just keep that end goal in mind!

EXERCISE NUMBER SEVENTEEN

The Fishbowl (with Friends)

This is a great exercise to do with a group of friends who also want to develop their superpowers! Here are the steps:

1. One person sits in "the hot seat" in the middle of "the fishbowl." He should have a pen and paper in hand. He says the name of his superhero alter ego and his main superpower. For example, "I am Capricorn the Planner, and my superpower is the power to strategize."

2. One person throws a question out to the person in the hot seat, and rather than answer the question, he just writes down the question. People in the group throw out more questions, so soon it seems as if the whole group is one entity, one school of fish. The person in the hot seat writes down questions as fast as he can. Please note: The questions can go from silly to serious. For example, "How do you deal with frenemies?" to "How would you handle a conflict between your personal and professional life?"

3. After a few minutes or until the person in the middle has enough questions to work with, the next person gets into the hot seat, and the pattern continues as before. Keep going until everyone has had a turn.

4. Afterward, set a timer for fifteen minutes.

5. Each person will try to answer the questions for themselves on the page. Afterward, each participant could choose one answer to share with the group. It's a way to really get to know your superhero, what he's been through, and what he's capable of!

MANTRA NUMBER ONE

Connect to your superpower through your mantra below.

Take at least one minute to say it out loud (but of course go as long as you wish). Shift your voice and energy each time. Perhaps the first time you say it in a neutral way. Then you say it super slow. Then you say it in a country and western accent. Next you whisper. Next you say it while laughing . . . you get the idea. Pay attention to how the words move through your body and how the mantra shifts your energy for the better. Mantras are less about words and more about the vibration of the words. You can also silently speak this mantra anytime. Just breathe into it and see what wondrous images, feelings, and ideas it helps you conjure up. As you practice this mantra, you will discover new associations with these words, so they feel fresh and relevant to your life.

Aries: I am Aries the Warrior, and I possess the power to act, so act I will!

Taurus: I am Taurus the Maker, and I possess the power to build, so build I will!

Gemini: I am Gemini the Messenger, and I possess the power to communicate, so communicate I will!

Cancer: I am Cancer the Guardian, and I possess the power to protect, so protect I will!

Leo: I am Leo the Leader, and I possess the power to inspire, so inspire I will!

Virgo: I am Virgo the Gardener, and I possess the power to cultivate, so cultivate I will!

Libra: I am Libra the Artist, and I possess the power to harmonize, so harmonize I will!

Scorpio: I am Scorpio the Shaman, and I possess the power to transform, so transform I will!

Sagittarius: I am Sagittarius the Traveler, and I possess the power to explore, so explore I will!

Capricorn: I am Capricorn the Planner, and I possess the power to strategize, so strategize I will!

Aquarius: I am Aquarius the Visionary, and I possess the power to invent, so invent I will!

Pisces: I am Pisces the Dreamer, and I possess the power to imagine, so imagine I will!

MANTRA NUMBER TWO

Discover Your Supermantra Sound

One of the spiritual as well as scientific laws of the universe is: Everything vibrates. We may not be able to see the vibratory movement with our eyes, but on a quantum level, this is what is happening. All matter is composed of fundamental particles that are in constant vibratory motion. Chanting "om," as you may do in a yoga class, comes from ancient Hindu rituals. In Kabbalah, every word contains a sacred energy that comes to life when we speak the word (as opposed to just reading it or thinking it).

Make sure you are in a space where you have privacy and will not be interrupted. Settle yourself into a trancelike state. Allow sounds to emit from your mouth. No regular words. Whatever sounds come out, follow them with other sounds. The idea is to free-associate with aural frequencies. You don't want to emit anything you have any association with—whether a word or a tune. You can utter syllables, but they cannot turn into words. If you do say a word or hum a known piece of music, no sweat, just move on.

When you find yourself coming back to a particular sound, begin to repeat it. Allow yourself to just feel the vibration of this sound. After a couple of minutes (or more if you wish), close your eyes and repeat the sound silently to yourself. Just keep repeating it.

When your mind starts to wander, keep coming back to this silent mantra in your mind. Don't worry if it comes out in different ways—slowly, quickly, quirkily, jerkily. Allow it to just keep coming back.

Now guess what? You have a mantra! Do not share it with anyone.

The ideal practice, inspired by transcendental meditation, will be to sit for twenty minutes two times a day, silently repeating your mantra to yourself. Of course, you should build up to this. Maybe five minutes one day. The next day, try five minutes twice a day, and so on until you hit the ideal. But whatever works for you is what you should do.

❋ MANTRA NUMBER THREE ❋

My High-Vibe Tribe Always Has My Back

Fill in your information in this template below:

"My High-Vibe Tribe always has my back. Thank you, ___ Sun. Thank you, ___ Moon. Thank you, ___ Rising. We are the all-stars."

It's short and sweet. You can write it on a note to keep on you, or on an index card to put by your bed. The key with this mantra is repetition. When you are feeling all alone, it is a wonderful way to remind yourself that you have friends, and those friends exist inside of you. Identifying each one of the three also makes them more familiar. You will start to sense them when they are around you at various times during your day, your week, your life, offering you guidance and support.

And the last thing to mention is the joy they bring out in you. Imagine if you were feeling lonely, rejected, or just off-kilter, and you ran into three of your besties. Wouldn't your mood immediately elevate?

❋ MEDITATION NUMBER ONE ❋

Walk the Path

Find a comfortable place where you will not be disturbed. Close your eyes and breathe in and out for a minute or two to calm your nervous system. When your mind wanders, just come back to the feeling of your inhalation and exhalation.

Imagine you are walking a pleasant country path. Lose yourself in peacefulness. You can smell the clean air, the flowers and trees. The sounds of birds chirping are pleasing to your ears. The ground feels solid and good under your feet. The trees protect you from the Sun, and everything feels lovely. Walk along for a couple of minutes, just enjoying your experience and immersing yourself in this pleasant environment.

As you walk along, imagine you see a large, hand-carved wooden bench at the end of the path. On it sits your Future Self. This is you, but the you who has fully accessed your superpowers. Sit down next to them and exchange greetings. What is it that you notice about them? What is the essence of the energy they put out?

Now ask them what steps they took to get where they are today.

Ask them what is one small step you can take now to move in that direction. Ask them a couple other questions you are wondering about. Thank them and walk back along the path.

❋ MEDITATION NUMBER TWO ❋

Animal Shape-Shifting

In the 2025 movie *Superman*, the Man of Steel has a Pet of Cute named Krypto. During this meditation you will encounter your animal sidekick. You can do this meditation again and again. Different animals will appear at different times, just when you need them!

1. Find a comfortable position, close your eyes, and breathe in and out, focusing on your inhalation and exhalation. When your mind starts to wander, just come back to your breath.

2. Imagine you are out somewhere in nature. Whatever environment comes to you is fine. It could be a forest, a nature trail, a beach, etc. Imagine you are walking along peacefully. You feel the need for companionship, and soon an animal appears. The animal may or may not be associated with this particular environment, but go with the flow. It's just a game.

3. Greet the animal and ask them if they have a message for you. If yes, listen to the message. If not, keep moving along until you see another animal who does have a message.

4. What does the message mean to you in your day-to-day life? Take a couple of minutes to free-associate. You may get words, images, or a sense of just knowing.

5. Now ask the animal if you can enter their body and feel what it's like to be them. Once you receive permission, imagine your etheric body entering the animal. In your mind you may see a "ghost" version

of you that moves into the animal. Now explore what it's like to be this animal. If it's a bird, perhaps you fly; a panther, you hunt; a kangaroo, you hop! Tune in to what it feels like to be this animal.

6. Now imagine that you, as the animal, are traveling alongside your superhero alter ego. What do you do together? What is your mission? How does your superhero self mix their superpowers with the animal's?

7. When you are ready to return to your human form, thank the animal and re-enter your own body. Ask yourself: What was the takeaway from this exercise? When you open your eyes, make a note of what came through and how you can use it in your real life.

MEDITATION NUMBER THREE

Connecting the Dots of Your Life

Relax and get into a comfortable position. Close your eyes. Breathe in and out for a minute or two, paying attention only to your inhalation and exhalation. When your mind wanders, just come back to the breath.

Imagine that you are entering the black void of space. Pull back the imaginary curtain of regular life and step into the void. This is the void of possibility. Nothing exists yet in manifested form, only as potential. Allow your body to dissipate into nothingness, so that all is left is energy. There is no "you" at the moment.

Then, using only the power of the universal mind, ask to

be shown the key events of your life—the rough ones as well as the wonderful ones. After a while, ask your superhero self to help you see the connections between these seemingly random, unconnected events in your life. Your superhero self can draw lines showing how one experience led to the next, then the next. Don't get too caught up in the details of the lines and numbers, though. Just try to see the big picture and ask your superhero self to help you understand what this seemingly random pattern means in terms of your life journey, why you are here on earth at this time, what path to follow . . .

Afterward, thank your superhero self and write down your takeaway for the exercise.

You got this!

THE FINAL KEY TO TRANSFORMING INTO A SUPERHERO

My Dear Readers,

When I first received a download from the universe instructing me to write this book, it was in anticipation of the Pluto in Aquarius era, which at that time was still a few years away. Today I planned to write an ending letter to you lovely readers, and whaddayaknow! I was awakened early to a download from the universe telling me what to write. Here it is:

During Pluto in Aquarius, as we create new social paradigms and invent new technologies, communication across our world becomes even more accessible, and we may even begin open contact with beings from alien worlds. We'd do well to simultaneously hold space for what awaits us during Pluto in Pisces, which begins approximately in 2043 and lasts until 2067.

As the **Aquarian Era of Invention** winds down, the **Piscean Era of Intuition** will begin. After many years of using our brains for discovery and innovation, we will be ready to reclaim our humanity, using a tool our species has always possessed: telepathy. Telepathy allows us to communicate our thoughts and feelings with each other directly, whether staring into each other's eyes or standing in silence and stillness on opposite ends of the globe. If this seems hard to imagine, think of it this way: Telepathy is just an extension of empathy. When we feel what is in a loved one's heart in *our own heart*, that's empathy. If the collective does this, it's mass empathy. Pluto in Pisces will be an era where we feel more connected to each other. Our relationships, on a personal level, will feel easier; we'll understand each other better. Imagine that level of understanding spreading out to the masses.

Just as we know through scientific discoveries of nonlocal quantum entanglement, as well as the way trees communicate through an underground network of fungi nicknamed the "wood wide web," we too possess this superpower. We have simply forgotten about it and grown to rely mainly on our aptitude for speech.

Now that you have come to the end of this book, you know I have woven in many ideas and exercises that revolve around ***you*** communicating with other parts of ***you***. The point of this is to integrate your discrete parts into a natural, elegant state of wholeness. That is the *micro* experience. The Pluto in Pisces era will be the *macro* experience where we all come back together as one.

So many of us feel disconnected from ourselves and from each other. During the Pluto in Pisces era, telepathy will become more normalized. It will be a beautiful step in our collective evolution. Think of telepathy like acupuncture. It wasn't so long ago that this healing modality was considered kooky alternative medicine. Now it's mainstream. And the funny thing is, acupuncture evolved from elements of traditional Chinese medicine, which has been around for thousands of years. Everything old is new again, and the same will be true for telepathy!

Pisces is the last sign of the zodiac, and as such it rules the last house in the horoscope chart: the twelfth. This is the house of endings and new beginnings. As we look to the future when Pluto will be transiting Pisces, it would behoove us to look to the past as well. As noted in this book's introduction, Indigenous peoples have long believed in the "dreamtime." Soon enough we will communicate frequently through dreams and telepathy, using symbols and feelings more than words.

This morning, when I was finishing notes on my download from the universe, I asked, "How should I end this letter to my readers?" As often happens for me, the universe advised me to close my eyes. When I did, I saw an image of a bear.

I associated this immediately with a story from Jamie Sams and David Carson's beautiful Native American Animal Medicine Cards. In the guide to these tarot cards, Sams and Carson write of Bear traveling to the Dream Lodge to access answers from the endless void of eternity, where a council of ancestors shares its wisdom. It made me think of Superman's Fortress of Solitude! After being shown this image of Bear, I shuffled my Animal Medicine Cards and pulled one at random. What do you think it was? Yep. Of course it was Bear; the universe speaks to us through synchronicity.

And so, dear readers, tonight, when you go to sleep, ask for a message from the universe and see what comes. If you make this a habit, you will begin to remember who you really are, who you always were, and who you always will be: **A SUPERHERO!**

With love,
Jill

ACKNOWLEDGMENTS

I want to thank Ellen Scordato, my agent at Stonesong, for her Sagittarian enthusiasm, largesse of spirit, and straight-to-the point advice. Thank you.

I am also grateful to my editors, Emma Peters and Ann Treistman, and the whole team at Countryman Press. You are all superheroes!

Joelle Hahn, your notes at a critical point in my process were incredibly helpful.

Finally, I must thank my clients. You inspire me.

INDEX

C

D

M

N

P

R

S

T